Blue Cats
and
Chartreuse Kittens

Blue Cats
and
Chartreuse Kittens

HOW SYNESTHETES COLOR
THEIR WORLDS

PATRICIA LYNNE DUFFY

A W. H. Freeman Book

TIMES BOOKS
HENRY HOLT AND COMPANY   NEW YORK

Times Books
Henry Holt and Company, LLC
Publishers since 1866
115 West 18th Street
New York, New York 10011

Henry Holt® is a registered trademark of
Henry Holt and Company, LLC.

Due to limitations of space, illustration credits can be found on page 185.

Library of Congress Cataloging-in-Publication Data
Duffy, Patricia Lynne, 1952–
   Blue cats and chartreuse kittens : how synesthetes color their worlds /
by Patricia Lynne Duffy; with a foreword by Peter Grossenbacher.
      p. cm.
ISBN 0-7167-4088-5
1. Synesthesia. 2. Color vision. 3. Perception. I. Title.
BF497 .D84 2001
152.1'89—dc21   2001002496

Henry Holt books are available for special promotions and
premiums. For details contact: Director, Special Markets.

First Edition 2001

Designed by Blake Logan

Printed in the United States of America

1   3   5   7   9   10   8   6   4   2

to the memory of my father,
Jack Duffy

The brain is wider than the sky,
For put them side by side
The one the other will contain with ease—
And you beside.

—EMILY DICKINSON

contents

a

foreword: more than a curiosity: synesthesia and the science of mind

"Until very recent years, it was supposed by philosophers that there was a typical human mind which all individual minds were like. . . . Lately however, a mass of revelations have poured in which make us see how false a view this is."

—WILLIAM JAMES, 1890

Over a century ago, William James, the father of American experimental psychology, observed that each mind has its own way of perceiving the world. Since then, psychological science has grown into a heavily researched field, and to this day, we continue to unearth more and more evidence that reveals the wisdom of James's observation. Indeed, it has become a hallmark not only of psychological research but of the value society places on diversity. In light of this, we should be especially interested in learning about one another's minds and our varied ways of perceiving the world. The chapters in this book share personal perspectives from those who experience synesthesia, a peculiar combining of sense perceptions, where sounds can have colors and tastes can have shapes. Persons with synesthesia might report "seeing" the "colors" of words or music, or "feeling" the "shapes" of tastes or touch sensations. Such persons (called "synesthetes") are not speaking metaphorically; rather, they are describing what is for them an everyday reality.

Although I do not experience synesthesia myself, I have conducted scientific research into this intriguing phenomenon since

1993. My strong interest in synesthesia was sparked by a series of conversations with Dr. Simon Baron-Cohen, while I was conducting postdoctoral research at Cambridge University in England, Dr. Baron-Cohen had already made several important discoveries about the nature of this rare sensory experience and challenged me to apply the methods and findings of cognitive neuroscience to synesthesia.

Since then, the work of many researchers has been amassed to provide substantial objective evidence that synesthesia happens (Grossenbacher and Lovelace, 2001). My own sustained commitment to this research is being carried out by two doctoral students, Christopher Lovelace and Carol Crane, who joined me at the National Institutes of Health to study synesthesia. Careful experimentation under controlled conditions in the laboratory has revealed psychological processes that match synesthetes' descriptions of their subjective experience.

On a purely scientific level, synesthesia provides a wonderful opportunity for learning how the different human senses of sight, hearing, smell, taste, and touch come together in the brain. Because we already know so much about how each sense works on its own, scientific exploration is now poised to better understand how the different senses interact with one another.

Upon first hearing about synesthesia, many people wonder whether they should believe what they hear. How could some people experience such fantastic blends of perceptions every day when most people have never experienced anything of the sort? To better understand this idea, it's worth considering a similar argument over another subjective sensory experience that was once viewed with great skepticism. Earlier in this century, there was great scientific debate over the existence of visual imagery. Visual imagery is the ability to consciously picture something in the mind's eye. Not all individuals think in images; some are unable to visualize a familiar scene if it is not actually in front of their eyes. On what basis could such people be sure that others really do experience visual imagery? The scientific debate over visual imagery was resolved when objective measures of behavior and physiology provided overwhelming evidence that visual imagery does occur. For example, scientists showed that the time taken to mentally move from one part of an image to another (like imagining first one room and then another in your home) depends on the distance between those parts of the imagined scene (Kosslyn, Ball, Reiser, 1978). This result revealed that visual imagery relies upon a mental representation of the spatial layout of a visual scene, just as in visual perception proper.

After determining that visual imagery really does happen, scientists wanted to know about brain events related to visual imagery. Positron emission tomography, or PET scanning, is a technologically advanced method of measuring the changes in blood flow that occur in each region of the brain during perception. Changes in blood flow indicate in turn how hard each part of the brain is working at a given time. Several physiological studies have used this PET technique to measure patterns of blood flow in the human brain during visual imagery, and recent studies have revealed a unique pattern of neural activity in the brains of those with synesthesia.

We can already imagine some of the possible applications that could follow from knowing more about the fascinating sensory anomaly of synesthesia. It is possible that the connections that exist in the brains of synesthetes may also exist—unused—in the brains of nonsynesthetes. If so, it may become possible to devise new methods of rehabilitation of stroke and other brain disorders. The idea would be to help a patient make use of the latent connections actively used by synesthetes.

This book is remarkable in that it describes the personal, inner experiences of different synesthetes. These introspections are fascinating in themselves, but they can also inspire every reader, whether experiencing synesthesia or not, to delve further into his or her own mind. Cultivating greater awareness is the only sure-fire way not to let the rich experience of life pass us by. I sincerely hope that reading about the mental life of synesthetes will inspire us to more deeply explore our own nature. In the epigraph above, William James pointed out the idiosyncratic nature of human minds. Only by comparing our own experience to that of other persons can we find out for ourselves whether James was correct.

Peter G. Grossenbacher, Ph.D.
National Institute of Mental Health
Bethesda, Maryland
July, 2000

prologue: 50 blue cats for dad

*The differences between men are profound, and we can
only be saved from living in blind unconsciousness of our
own mental peculiarities by the habit of informing ourselves
as well as we can of those of others.*

—SIR FRANCIS GALTON,
INQUIRIES INTO THE HUMAN FACULTY

I was sixteen when I found out. The year was 1968. My father and
I were in the kitchen—he, in his usual talk-spot by the pantry
door, my sixteen-year-old self in a chair by the window. The two of us
were reminiscing about the time I was a little girl, learning to write the
letters of the alphabet. We remembered that, under his guidance, I'd
learned to write all of the letters very quickly except for the letter R.

"Until one day," I said to my father, "I realized that to make an R
all I had to do was first write a P and then draw a line down from its
loop. And I was so surprised that I could turn a yellow letter into an
orange letter just by adding a line."

"Yellow letter? Orange letter?" my father said. "What do you
mean?"

"Well, you know," I said. "P is a yellow letter, but R is an orange
letter. You know—the colors of the letters."

"The colors of the letters?" my father said.

It had never come up in any conversation before. I had never
thought to mention it to anyone. For as long as I could remember,
each letter of the alphabet had a different color. Each word had a different color, too (generally, the same color as its first letter), and so

did each number. The colors of letters, words, and numbers were as intrinsic a part of them as their shapes, and like the shapes, the colors never changed. They appeared automatically whenever I saw or thought about letters or words, and I couldn't alter them.

I had taken it for granted that the whole world shared these perceptions with me, so my father's perplexed reaction was totally unexpected. From my point of view, I felt as if I'd made a statement as ordinary as "apples are red" and "leaves are green" and had elicited a thoroughly bewildered response. I didn't know then that perceiving such things as yellow P's and orange R's or green B's, purple 5's, brown Mondays, and turquoise Thursdays was unique to the one in two thousand persons like myself who were hosts to a quirky neurological phenomenon called "synesthesia." In synesthesia, when one of the five senses is stimulated, both that one *plus* another sense responds. This can lead "synesthetes" to experience such peculiarly blended perceptions as words and sounds having colors or even tastes having shapes. Later in my life, I would read about such synesthetes as Michael Watson (whom neurologist Dr. Richard Cytowic writes about in his book *The Man Who Tasted Shapes*), for whom the taste of a well-cooked chicken triggered the feeling of something pointy sitting in his hand, while an undercooked one triggered the feeling of something disappointingly round. Another synesthete described the name "Francis" as having "the taste of baked beans"; yet another, artist Carol Steen, says serious headaches are "an overpowering orange," while mild ones are "just green." I would also read of neuroscientists' explanations of such phenomena: In the last decade or so, those working at England's Cambridge University have done studies indicating that synesthesia could be passed through the genes, producing an unusual patterning of neurons in synesthetes' brains and causing sight to cross with sound, taste to cross with touch.

But that day in the kitchen, my father and I, never having heard of synesthesia, both felt bewildered. My father's bewilderment increased when he learned that his daughter saw not only colored letters, but also colored numbers and colored time: A week was a colored sidewalk with seven squares of pavement, one for each day, and a year was an oblong string of twelve colored rectangles. My father felt surprised at my descriptions of these, and I felt surprised at his surprise. For me, it was one of those coming-of-age moments when I glimpsed that the world might not really be as I had grown up perceiving it. It was a moment when that most basic of questions that binds human beings socially—"Do you see what I see?"—seemed to hang in a vacuum, independent of any shared context.

I suddenly felt marooned on my own private island of navy blue C's, dark brown D's, sparkling green 7's, and wine-colored V's. What else did I see differently from the rest of the world? I wondered. What did the rest of the world see that I didn't? It occurred to me that maybe every person in the world had some little oddity of perception they weren't aware of that put them on a private island, mysteriously separated from others. I suddenly had the dizzying feeling that there might be as many of these private islands as there were people in the world.

That conversation in the kitchen propelled my father to look high and low in libraries and bookstores, searching for some bit of information to explain his daughter's peculiar perceptions. His search led to synesthesia, the magic word that put my perceptions on the map of recognized terrain of human experience. He found the reference to synesthesia in a used bookstore copy of *Yoga Digest*, in an article about meditation. My father and I were later to find that others, too, had traveled synesthetic terrain: Nineteenth-century French poet Arthur Rimbaud wrote a sonnet, "Voyelles," about seeing colored vowels; one of the greatest twentieth-century novelists, Vladimir Nabokov, described his colored alphabet in his autobiography, *Speak, Memory*; composers Franz Liszt and Olivier Messiaen both saw colored musical notes (Liszt was reported to have instructed an orchestra, "Gentlemen, a little bluer if you please," and Messiaen celebrated his colored music in compositions such as "The Colors of Time"); painter David Hockney describes how hearing "colored music" helped him design stage sets for the Metropolitan Opera; artist Carol Steen expresses her synesthetic perceptions in sculpture and painting; and physicist Richard Feynman described the colored equations he "saw" in formulating the quantum theory that earned him a Nobel prize.

Minds far less awesome have experienced the world synesthetically, but those who possess them tend to keep silent about their perceptions since they feel inhibited by the fact that so many people have neither experienced nor heard of synesthesia. We synesthetes learn early on that to most people, our perceptions are merely quirky, even suspect. Other people don't see what we see and they're not convinced that we see it ourselves. But what each of us sees is the reality we know, and we are not at liberty to change it. I am no more able to change the white color of the letter O than I am to change its circular shape; for me, the one is as much an attribute of the letter as the other. For a synesthete, the colors of letters, numbers, or musical notes are not arbitrary. They are just there, part and parcel of the thing they help to make visible in the world.

For centuries, scientists didn't know what to make of the strange reports of synesthetes. With only anecdotal evidence to go on, their attempts at scientific research came to a near halt. Even nineteenth-century scientist Sir Francis Galton, who actually devoted much of his time to the study of reports of synesthetic perceptions, initially proclaimed, "One of these accounts is more lunatic than the next." Now that science has the technology to look inside the brain and observe its activity, the study of synesthesia has resumed. These days, scientists at major universities and institutes—such as the Pierce Laboratory at Yale University, MIT, the National Institutes of Health, and Cambridge University—who are eager to know the secrets synesthesia may yield about the human brain, are looking into synesthetes' brains with high-tech scanners.

Back in 1993, my husband Josh happened across an article on some of this recent synesthesia research in, of all places, *The Economist* magazine. Casually passing the piece to me, he asked, "Isn't this what you told me you have?" The article, titled "Purple Prose" (written by Alison Motluck, herself a synesthete), told of research at the Institute of Psychiatry in London, where Dr. Simon Baron-Cohen headed a team of neuroscientists who were finding that something different really was happening in the brains of synesthetes. I promptly wrote to Dr. Baron-Cohen, and even made a "pilgrimage" to London to meet him that very next summer. Over tea in his office in London's Denmark Hill, Dr. Baron-Cohen told me how colored-language synesthetes processed language and sounds in a part of their brains normally reserved for processing visual information. He also introduced me to the International Synesthesia Association (ISA), which had sponsored one-day conferences with presentations by synesthetes and researchers. I quickly became a member of ISA, and several years later, I went to England to attend one of its conferences held at Cambridge University.

At the Cambridge meeting, about fifty synesthetes gathered to hear presentations in which our perceptions were clothed in the dignified garb of scientific "findings." Researchers reported that synesthetes' descriptions share common features: For a great many, a word takes on the color cast of its first letter; almost all see the letters O, I, and U in the same color range (white, white to pale gray, and yellow to light brown, respectively). We also learned that a possible genetic basis for synesthesia was being studied, as the phenomenon tended to cluster in families. Researchers told us that by studying synesthesia they hoped to gain more insight into the mysterious workings of the human brain and perhaps into the ways in which all people, synesthete and non-synesthete, filter their perceptions and "color" their worlds.

As synesthetes chatted during the tea-and-biscuit reception at Cambridge's elegant Old Combination Room, all felt elated. "I feel validated" was the most-heard phrase. Here were people who'd been told for years by family, friends, and colleagues that their colored-sounds perceptions were "silly," "flaky," or, worse still, "made up." Most had long ago given up sharing such perceptions with others. As one soft-spoken, middle-aged Cambridge woman confessed to me, "As a child, when I first mentioned that everyone's name had a color, I was told I must be very stupid or very foolish to say such things." As an adult, she was thrilled to be part of the university's research on synesthesia.

The sense of relieved self-validation most felt that day is not surprising when we consider how much hangs on the question "Do you see what I see?": whom we will marry, who our friends and allies at the office will be. It is one of the basic questions that propel us through life, leading us to share some of our most intimate moments with other people, reinforcing our sense of who we are and what the world is.

At home in New York, away from the gathering of synesthetes, I turn to the Internet, that great validator of nonstandard perception. As I log on to MIT's synesthesia Web site, I realize I am resuming that conversation I had with my father back in 1968.

Long before the Internet existed and long before prestigious universities dignified the study of synesthesia with conferences and Web sites, my father, all by himself, validated what I saw. Because he was convinced there was some internal logic to his daughter's unusual perceptions, he willingly engaged in that suspension of disbelief required for one vision to open to another.

Some months ago, I was going through a drawer in that same kitchen where my father and I had had our conversation about my colored alphabet so many years before. I came across a drawing I had done at the age of seven titled "50 Blue Cats for Dad." On the back of it, in an added note dated 5/68, my father had written: "Update on Patty's art work: She just told me today that 'cat' is a blue word. Now I understand why these cats are blue." (See page 98.)

chapter one

DRAWING COLORED WORDS
FOR MY FATHER

Colors hide within everything, including the night.

—KATHERINE VAZ, SAUDADE

As far back as I can remember, letters of the alphabet, numbers, and words have been in color. But I also remember that in my preliterate days, before I knew how to read or write, each word evoked, in my mind's eye, its own unique and unchanging colorful design. Sometimes I drew pictures of the word-designs I "saw" and showed them, as I did all of my pictures, to my father.

At that time, my father was home a lot. First, he took off from work to look after his own father who had fallen into a depression born of old age and illness. Later, when his father died, my father fell into a depression himself. In the gray decade of the 1950s, fathers were not supposed to be home too much or fall into depressions. My mother told me that I cheered my father up. I think our experiments with color helped.

I remember my father sitting in the big, sagging green living room chair, his elbow on its arm, his chin in his hand. I would tug at that hand with my four-year-old insistence, bent on asking him questions about my crayons. I needed a color that was not in my crayon box. What could I do? When I was little, I drew a lot of pictures, and crayons played a big role in my life. At my insistence, my father let himself be pulled up out of his drab green overstuffed chair and over to my bright, shiny little red table where, every day, I drew all kinds of pictures. The little child's table was always overflowing with drawing paper and crayons of all different colors, sizes, and shapes. "But I don't have pink," I told my father, "and I need pink." The color pink was important that day. I was drawing a picture of a word—I don't remember now which word it was—but I remember it had a lot of pink in its word-design.

I liked drawing the different word-designs that appeared in my mind's eye when I heard words spoken. I never thought to tell anyone that these drawings were pictures of words. They were just my "designs." The designs were very consistent, each incorporating a whole array of shapes and colors, like patterns in a kaleidoscope. The word I was drawing that day had a lot of pink in its pattern.

"If you don't have pink," my father said, "maybe you can use your red crayon. And just color very lightly so it's almost like pink."

"No," I said. "I need pink."

My father looked fatigued. At that time, he didn't always sleep well at night and often looked tired all day. For a moment, I thought he was going to leave me to go back to his chair in the living room. But I needed help with colors, so I knew he would stay.

"I need pink, Daddy," I said again.

"Well," my father said, "Maybe we can make pink with your red crayon and your white crayon."

"Make pink?" I asked.

"Yes," my father said. "Putting two colors together makes a whole new color."

"A whole new color?" I repeated in wonder. "We can make pink?" It sounded magical. My child's awe held my father there by my little red table and kept him from returning to his gray-green chair. He even proposed we go into the kitchen to do a color experiment, making new crayons with new colors by melting down and recombining the colored crayons in my crayon box.

In the kitchen, sunlight streamed in through the window that looked out on the backyard cherry tree where birds perched and pecked on tiny red cherries. I watched with great excitement as my father grated crayons with my mother's vegetable grater. Vivid red and white crayon flakes fell from the grater into the pot on the stove as sparrows chirped and shadows from the backyard cherry tree fluttered around us on the walls of the kitchen. My father turned on the stove jet flame, and I watched in wonder as crayon flakes became crayon liquid, which he poured into an empty metal ballpoint pen holder and put into the oven. When it had "incubated" in the oven long enough, he removed it, opened up the penholder and, like a chick hatching, a new pink crayon was born—a bit awkward in its shape, but a usable pink crayon nonetheless.

I was thrilled. I danced in the kitchen sunlight with my new pink crayon.

"Can we make more colors?" I asked, wanting my father to stay with me in the sunlit kitchen.

We repeated the experiment, combining different crayon colors to make new colors. Sometimes, while waiting for this or that crayon to bake, I noticed my father looking sad, staring into the depths of something I couldn't see. But then I tugged at his hand and insisted it was time to "see more rainbow colors" and make more crayons. My father got up and melted a Crayola yellow and an evergreen together to bake a chartreuse, then melted a yellow and a red to bake a sunshine orange.

An idea came to me: If we could make such wonderful new colors by melting just two crayons together, imagine the magnificent color we could make if we combined all the different-colored crayons. I asked my father if we could make a crayon composed of all the colors in my crayon box.

He hesitated for a moment, then said, "Well, we'll do an experiment. We'll see what happens." Then he grated and melted together all the rest of my crayons, making multicolored crayon confetti, which then became swirls of colored liquid in the pot. After pouring this liquid into a pen holder we waited because, my father said, "This one will take longer to bake." He went into the living room and sat in his chair.

"Daddy, Daddy, come and see the rainbow colors, come and see the rainbow colors!" I kept chanting as I ran back and forth between the living room and the kitchen.

After some time, my father let me tug him back to the kitchen stove. He took the pen holder out of the oven and opened it; to my amazed disappointment, what hatched was not the one magnificent "rainbow color" I had expected, but simply a plain black crayon.

"Daddy why?" I asked him. "Why just black?"

"When you put all the different colors together," my father said, gently, seeing my disappointment, "you get black."

My child's mind connected the promising swirls of color turning black to my father's sadness.

For the rest of the day, I sat at my little red table, furiously coloring with my black crayon, filling sheet after sheet of drawing paper with black backgrounds on which I drew my brightly colored word-designs. Actually, this was how the word-designs appeared in my mind's eye: as luminous, colorful kaleidoscopic patterns, appearing out of blackness, evoked by the sounds of words.

Later that day, I showed my father all the colorful designs I had drawn with my crayons; it never occurred to me to tell him they were pictures of words. They were just "my designs." I remember very much liking the sound of the word "design" and drawing a picture of it, too. But now I have only the vaguest memory of what that, or any of these word-designs, looked like.

People have asked me why, as a child, I didn't mention my colored words to anyone. It never dawned on me to talk about them. They were just part of the world I was discovering. At that age, different occurrences were inextricably woven together to create a single pattern of lived experience. It never occurred to me to break that pattern down, describing the designs that appeared in my mind as if they were something unusual. Seeing designs had always been part of my experience of hearing words, and it didn't occur to me to wonder whether other people heard words as colorful designs. I just thought the designs in my mind were pretty, and I wanted to draw them to make my father happy. (See page 83.)

Now, however, the pretty word-designs exist only as faint memories. According to some researchers, including Yale University's Dr. Lawrence Marks, many children who experience strong synesthesia in childhood lose it in adulthood, although for one in two thousand of us, it remains. The reason for this could be, in part, physiological. As the brain matures, it clearly delineates its sensory responses into "this is sight," "this is sound," "this is smell," "this is taste," and "this is touch." The sensory responses no longer overlap. But the still immature brains of babies seem to operate very differently. Researcher Daphne Maurer tells us that all babies under the age of four months have synesthetic responses because the brain has not yet differentiated its functions into discrete compartments that respond separately to a stimulus that is visual, auditory, olfactory, gustatory, or tactile. The young infant does not segregate experience into discrete sensory components. In an article titled "Neonatal Synesthesia," Maurer says, "A newborn's senses are not well differentiated, but instead are intermingled in a synesthetic confusion." In their book *The World of the Newborn*, Daphne and Charles Maurer describe the young infant's sensory experience this way:

His world smells to him much as our world smells to us, but he does not perceive odors as coming through his nose alone. He hears odors, and sees odors, and feels them too. His world is a melee of pungent aromas—and pungent sounds and bitter-smelling sounds, and sweet-smelling sights and sour-smelling pressures against the skin. If we could visit the newborn's world, we would think ourselves inside a hallucinatory perfumery.

Young infants perceive total patterns of energy, rather than discrete patterns filtered through one or another of the five senses.

In time, however, the brain develops and compartmentalizes its functions, and the synesthetic fusion of infancy gives way to the discrete sensory experiences of later childhood and adulthood. One theory about why some adults have one or another form of synesthesia is that the segregation of functions doesn't fully take place in the brains of some people. This incomplete development process thus causes the brain to take in sensory experience in a partially blended way, sound fusing with sight, sight fusing with touch, touch fusing with taste, taste fusing with shape, according to the individual. A whole range of synesthetic experiences is possible, and for centuries, reports of these have found their way not only into scientific journals, but also into poems, novels, and even children's books.

A synesthetic fusion of sound and taste is represented imaginatively by Norton Juster in his well-known children's book *The Phantom Toll Booth*. One chapter describes a marketplace where binfuls of alphabet letters are sold. Shoppers buy the letters in order to make words, but also in order to *taste* them. As the "letter man" who sells the letters tells the character Milo:

"Here taste an 'A'; they're very good."

Milo nibbled carefully at the letter and discovered that it was quite sweet and delicious—just the way you'd expect an 'A' to taste.

"I knew you'd like it," laughed the letter man, popping two G's and an 'R' into his mouth and letting the juice drip down his chin. "A's are one of our most popular letters. All of them aren't that good," he confided in a low voice. "Take the Z for instance—very dry and sawdusty. And the X? Why, it tastes like a trunkful of stale air. . . . But most of the others are quite tasty. . . ."

Could it be that such synesthetic descriptions ring familiar to young readers because they themselves experienced such perceptual blendings in the not-so-distant past of their infanthood?

In 1980, researchers David Lewkowicz and Gerry Turkewitz conducted studies revealing that young infants make no distinction between visual and auditory stimuli, but only in the intensity of stimuli, regardless of their type. In one of these experiments, one-month-old babies made no distinction between a flash of light and a burst of white noise of comparable intensity. Measures of the babies' heart rates indicated they reacted as if to a single stimulus, responding only to changes in intensity; it did not matter whether the change in intensity was in the light or the noise, for the two were experienced by the babies as a single stimulus. As long as the light or the noise remained at comparable levels of intensity, the babies' heart rates would also remain at constant levels. But if the intensity of either light or sound increased or decreased, the babies' heart rates would change in response. A change in the *type* of stimulus alone—for example, visual to auditory—produced no change in the babies' responses. This outcome surprised the experimenters because it is quite different from the way older children or adults would respond. Older children and adults exhibit one distinct response to seeing light and another to hearing sound; heart rates will change in response to a change in sensory mode, regardless of whether these different modes of stimuli have matching levels of intensity. But the babies in the experiment responded as if they'd been presented with a single sensory stimulus, although one was light and the other sound.

Just as young babies experience life as a sensory blend, young children experience life as an integrated pattern and don't think to question, but simply to live. Children have experiences they accept and don't describe to adults. This is why many parents never know if their child experiences synesthesia and why many people with synesthesia don't learn that their form of perception is unusual until they reach adulthood; in some cases, synesthetes probably go through life never becoming aware that their perceptions differ from the norm.

Some synesthetes report that synesthesia becomes less intense on reaching adulthood. Why can I no longer remember my word-designs? I think they began to disappear when I started to learn the alphabet, the socially endorsed representation of language. I remember at age three or four being fascinated by written words and alphabet letters I saw on the coffee jars and cereal boxes on our kitchen table. I sat there with a pencil, copying them onto drawing paper as if they were designs. I copied "Maxwell House Coffee: Good to the last drop" from its red-labeled jar and "Jane Parker Apple Pie: Mouth watering good" from its flat blue-and-white box. I couldn't read the words I was copying; at that age, I could read alphabet letters, but almost no words. I remember wanting more than anything to be old enough to go to school so I could learn to read the words I was copying. My father and mother encouraged this copying of words and letters, and I remember they always sang the alphabet song with me as I copied. For the longest time, singing the song "A-B-C-D-E-F-G/ -H-I-J-K/-LMNO/-P" gave me the idea that "LMNO" was the name of a single letter. I remember both my parents laughing when I asked, "How do you write an LMNO?" And I still remember that, in my mind's eye, the "LMNO" took the form of an abstract design, reminiscent of an angular yellow and brown bird with a triangular beak.

All the alphabet letters I learned had color right away. I wonder sometimes if there was any connection between the colors in my original word-designs and the colors evoked by the sounds of alphabet letters. I wish I could recall the word-designs well enough to compare the colors. I do know that the letters L, M, N, and O are, respectively, yellow, brown, dark brown, and white, much like the color of the bird-like shape I saw in my mind's eye at the sound of "LMNO."

For some reason, it took me a very long time to draw the letter R. I tried again and again, but just couldn't get the hang of it. My father, seeing my frustration, patiently demonstrated and redemonstrated the way to draw it, but I just couldn't seem to imitate it. Then one day, staring for a long time at R, I noticed how similar in form it was to P. The only difference between the two letters was that a slanted line came down from P's "head." This meant that if I could make a P,

I *could* make an R! Excited, I held my breath as I picked up my pencil and made a P, then drew a slanted line down from its loop. And my theory worked—I had drawn an R! And unlike the light yellow of P, its color was orange. I marveled that a yellow letter could become an orange letter just by drawing a line!

"Daddy, Daddy, come and look, I made R!" My father hurried over to my little red table. There amidst the piles of word-design drawings and pages of penciled alphabet letters was my R: a little wobbly looking, perhaps, with lines that were more crooked than straight, but indisputably an R. My father broke into a big smile and, happy for me, happy that his instruction had taken effect, lifted me onto his shoulders to celebrate the success with a piggy-back ride.

As we pranced around the little red table, my eyes fell on our homemade black crayon, no longer the disappointing eraser of all colors, but simply their hiding place.

chapter two

THE DEVELOPING CHILD AND THE VARIETIES OF SYNESTHETIC EXPERIENCE

A Black, E White, I Red, U Green, O Blue: vowels
One day I will crack your nascent origins . . .

—ARTHUR RIMBAUD, "VOYELLES"

I still remember the thrill of having learned every letter of the alphabet. Finally learning to write that letter R made me feel initiated into the world older children and adults were part of—that mysterious place they all journeyed to every day, leaving their houses with schoolbags and briefcases. Mastering all the alphabet symbols was like knowing all the steps on the path that led to that mysterious world of the big people. I now felt it was only a matter of a short time before I would follow them into that world.

On my block, I was the youngest child, the only one not yet in school. I spent solitary hours trying to amuse myself from 8:30 A.M. to 3:30 P.M., drawing pictures at my little red table, taking solitary rides up and down the block on my training-wheel bicycle, copying words spelled out in their colorful alphabet letters from cans, jars, and boxes at the kitchen table.

I was enthralled with the alphabet, which I realize in retrospect gradually began to replace the colorful designs that would appear in my head whenever I heard words. In place of those designs, words written out in their different-colored letters began to appear. The alphabet's letter-shapes eventually replaced my word-designs, but the colors I "heard" stayed.

Several researchers have noted that synesthesia is far more common in children than in adults, with between one-third to one-half of children reporting such perceptions. Even as far back as 1883, neurologist G. Stanley Hall discovered that twenty-one out of fifty-three children he studied described the sounds of musical instruments as having colors. Hungarian scientist Geza Revesz, who studied the psychology of music and art, said in 1923 that nearly half of all children reported sound-color perceptions. But researchers have also noted that children who experience strong synesthesia often lose some elements of it along the journey to adulthood. Yale University researcher Lawrence Marks writes in his essay "On Colored Hearing Synesthesia":

Why does synesthesia tend to be lost with age? Probably because it is replaced by another, more flexible mode of cognition (i.e., abstract language). . . . [A]s the child matures and cognitive development ensues, it becomes valuable, indeed necessary, for the child to transfer the meanings from the perceptual-synesthetic to the verbal realm.

As the developing child takes his or her place within the community, the shared symbols of language are learned and the personal imagery of synesthesia begins to disappear or to be greatly diminished. However, while I have only a vague memory of all the many word-designs I used to "hear," the colors of the letters on my "alphabet trail" have retained their vividness. In my mind's eye, I see the colored alphabet letters as a place I go to get the letters I need. The letters are side by side on an upwardly sloping pathway, which I "glide" along in order to find the ones I need when spelling a word. The colors have not changed since I started learning to write, copying letters before I could even read the words they spelled.

Sometimes I would sit in front of the television with a pencil and paper, copying words that flashed on the screen during commercials:

"Campbell's soups are mm-m good, mm-m good," "Get Spic'n'Span!" "Mr. Clean, Mr. Clean!" I liked hearing the words and seeing them written out in the magical new letters I was learning. My father and I would sit together in front of the TV, and he would smile and even laugh when he observed how excited I became at seeing the words flash on the screen and how determined I was to copy them as fast as I could before they disappeared. He would use the occasion of our sitting together in front of the black-and-white Emerson television for a lesson in science, in the wonder of how things worked. "Isn't it amazing, Patty," he would say to me, "how a television set works!" Back in the 1950s when television was a new technology, it undoubtedly inspired the same sense of awe that advanced computer technology does today. But the workings of things had always inspired in my father a true sense of wonder, a bright light gleaming through the darker periods of his life. "Do you know," my father would say, "that the pictures we see on the TV screen are really made by just one little dot of light going back and forth and back and forth on the screen so fast that you can't see it moving?—You can just see the pictures it makes. Isn't it amazing?"

That did, indeed, seem amazing to me, but the idea of many wondrous things mysteriously contained in one very simple thing had already been introduced to me by the "black crayon experiment." If all the different colors in my crayon box could be concealed in a single black crayon, it seemed equally plausible to me that all the different scenes and situations on the TV screen could be hiding in a single white dot of light.

And so now, many years later, reading the research that synesthesia and its host of unique and varied perceptions may be the product of a single gene (interacting with others in the human genome) seems parallel to the black crayon and the white dot in being both wondrous and plausible. The variety of synesthetic experiences people describe is overwhelming. Seeing letters in color is only one form of synesthesia (albeit the most common form, almost a "garden variety"). And even within that one garden variety, the range of reported perceptions is staggering. Researchers who work with synesthetes often express amazement at the effort their subjects will make in order to show the precise subtleties of their letter or number colors. As National Institute of Mental Health researcher Chris Lovelace remarked, "It's not just blue, it's *that* blue with this or that highlight in it and a whole other color around its edges." In his book *Synesthesia: A Union of the Senses,* neurologist Dr. Richard Cytowic points out that taking great pains to describe the precise color of a letter or other sound-induced photism is a hallmark of synesthetes' descriptions. Dr. Cytowic writes, "Synesthesia seems to express itself in coding abstract knowledge in a very precise and very idiosyncratic way. The visualized system created by synesthesia may also sometimes serve to reveal some new properties of knowledge."

The following are some examples of letter and word colors reported by synesthetes.

In an essay, "Two Synaesthetes Talking Color," synesthete and science writer Alison Motluck describes

the glorious cherry red of an 'S' . . . the buffed black of an 'R' . . . the ugly powdery pale blue of the letter 'P,' the splendid rich purple of 'V.' . . . 'I' and 'O' are distinctly white and 'U' is yellow-ochre, the color of a particular shade of oil paint. I remember more than a decade ago . . . recognizing the color of 'U' in a tube of dirty-yellow-colored paint.

Emily Florian, a contributor to the Internet's synesthesia list, says, "'A' is like a dark red apple's skin or like blood; 'B' is paper-bag brown with a rather dull, mud-like surface like wet sand; 'E' is between the yellow of sunflower petals and ripe lemons (it is so strong, it makes my whole name shine yellow)." Ann Kennedy, an educator and textbook writer with a Ph.D. in linguistics, said in an interview, "L is very soft, light, meringue-like yellow. It's puffy." Carol Steen, an artist who paints and sculpts her synesthetic perceptions, claims, "The letter A is bright pink like the spun sugar of cotton candy; B is the color of a black sheep (which is not quite black); C is the blue of Jamaican waters; D is a cool, smoky gray, E is lipstick red . . . (and it doesn't stop there)."

A French language instructor at the United Nations who grew up in Paris, Anna Muir remembers her primary school teacher reading Rimbaud's poem "Voyelles" ("Vowels") to the class. In the poem, Rimbaud describes vowels as having colors. Anna realized that she had her own colors for each vowel and they were different from those in the poem. As she told me:

The poem said A was black, but for me it was pink. Most of my other vowel colors were different from Rimbaud's too. His E was white, but mine was blue; his I was red, while mine was yellow; both of our U's were green. So I assumed everyone had colors for vowels—just different ones from mine in most cases.

Another French synesthetic vision is described in Marcel Proust's novel *Remembrance of Things Past*. The narrator, Marcel, says that for him, the French surname "Guermantes" was always "suffused by [an] orange tint."

Synesthetes' descriptions of what they "see" have not changed much in the last two centuries they've been recorded. In 1883, in his book *Inquiries into the Human Faculty*, Sir Francis Galton reported an interview with a Dr. James Key, who asserted: "I have never been destitute in all my conscious existence of a conviction that 'E' is a clear cold light-gray blue. The letter 'R' has been invariable of a copper color, in which a swarthy blackness seems to intervene, visually corresponding to the trilled pronunciation of 'R.'"

Richard Feynman, who won the 1965 Nobel Prize in Physics, was also a synesthete. In his autobiography, *What Do You Care What Other People Think?*, Feynman gave this description:

When I see equations, I see the letters in colors—I don't know why. As I'm talking, I see vague pictures of Bessel functions from Jahnke's and Emede's book, with light-tan j's, slightly violet-bluish n's and dark brown x's flying around. And I wonder what the hell it must look like to the students.

In their book *Sparks of Genius: Thinking Tools of the World's Most Creative People*, Robert and Michele Root-Bernstein speculate that synesthetic perception may allow for a different approach to thinking about complex issues. Synesthetic thinking has the advantage of rendering abstract concepts into a form that is concrete, and so may allow for a unique way of considering some of the generally "ungraspable" scientific, artistic, and philosophical questions.

Some synesthetes describe not only colors but also tactile features of letters. Writer Vladimir Nabokov, author of some of the best novels and stories of the twentieth century, was particularly eloquent when describing his alphabet letters. In his autobiography, *Speak, Memory*, Nabokov tells us he "presents a fine case of colored hearing" and writes:

. . . a French a evokes polished ebony. This black group [of letters] also includes hard g (vulcanized rubber) and y (a sooty rag being ripped). Oatmeal n, noodle-limp l, and the ivory-backed hand mirror of o take care of the whites. I am puzzled by my French on which I see as the brimming tension-surface of alcohol in a small glass. Passing on to the blue group, there is steely x, thundercloud z, and huckleberry k. . . . I hasten to complete my list before I am interrupted. In the green group, there are alder-leaf f, the unripe apple of p, and pistachio t. Dull green, combined somehow with violet, is the best I can do for w. The yellows comprise various e's and i's, creamy d, bright golden y and u, whose alphabetical value I can express only by "brassy with an olive sheen." In the brown group, there are the rich, rubbery tone of soft g, paler j, and the drab shoelace of h. Finally, among the reds, b has the tone called burnt sienna by painters, m is a fold of pink flannel, and today I have at last perfectly matched v with "Rose Quartz" in Maerz and Paul's Dictionary of Color. . . .

Like Nabokov, Russian linguist Natasha Lvovich also reports a shift in the colors and tactile qualities of words in different languages. In her book *The Multilingual Self*, Lvovich describes how the colors and tactile qualities vary in the different languages she speaks: "In English, 'six' is whitish, fuzzy, dull glass; in French, creamy in color and substance. [Monday] in French, *Lundi*, is pale, wax pink; [Monday] in Russian, *Pondel'nik*, is grayish and dull, and [English] Monday is an orange-red-brown gamma." Natasha's fifteen-year-old daughter, Pauline, also a synesthete, reports that her Monday is orange. Mother and daughter, who are fluent in both Russian and English, report that letters of the Russian and English alphabets are similar if their sounds are similar. Natasha describes the English L sound as a "tough, very glassy, upfront pink, while the softer Russian L ('lya') sound is a soft, warm pink." For daughter Pauline, English L is blue, while Russian "lya" is a paler white-blue. When it comes to foreign languages, British artist and synesthete Elizabeth Stewart-Jones reports in an essay, "Two Synaesthetes Talking Color," that "French words are more apt to be dark, in blues and blacks and purples. Italian words show up more in brick-yellows."

In my own case, in languages other than English that use a Roman alphabet, I experience only a very subtle shift in the colors of letters. The tints of the letter-colors of French words, for example, are generally lighter and "airier" than they are for English words. However, in both languages, the letters share the same tactile qualities. My letter Z, for example, is a very, very dark brown with lines of bubbles inside. The "carbonation" of the Z is created by the buzzing of the "z-z-z-z" sound. The letter S is a sparkly white, the sparkles resulting from the "s-s-s" sound. The letter C, however, doesn't have any sparkles, perhaps because it ends with the solid vowel sound of E (although the same could be said of Z, which nevertheless has bubbles). The letter G is black with glints of yellow in it. I can't figure out why the yellow glints are there; it's just the way G looks.

Some synesthetes, like my friend Ann Kennedy, a linguist and writer, say that letters and language have an "active feeling":

This active feeling I have for things . . . like art . . . is also true about foreign languages, especially Italian . . . but it happens in Greek too. I "feel" the word first. . . . I physically have a reaction to the word I'm trying to come up with. In addition to feeling the word, I also get hints as to the color of the word.

Synesthetes who are native speakers of languages with non-Roman alphabets also report seeing the characters of the languages' writing systems in color. Shibana Tajwar, an environmental engineer who is a speaker of Bengali and Urdu, says that the colors of sounds in both languages correspond to similar sounds in English, although the shades may vary. Bengali's aspirated C sound is lemon-yellow like its English counterpart, but Bengali's unaspirated C is a paler yellow, "less lemon-y," as Shibana puts it. She describes the four different T sounds in Bengali and Urdu as having four different shades of blue. The Bengali T sound that resembles English T is navy blue. Similarly, Su Kim, a native speaker of Korean, reports that the Korean "ka" sound (ㄱ) is navy blue and has a rough texture, just like the English consonant K.

The colors that synesthetes experience for their alphabets tend to be very consistent. The usual "test" for colored-letter synesthesia is to ask a synesthete to identify all of his or her colored-letter correspondences. Then, some time later, without warning, the synesthete is called into the lab to tell his or her colored-letter correspondences once again. In one such experiment performed in 1993 by Dr. Simon Baron-Cohen at the Institute of Psychiatry in London, 92 percent of synesthetes identified the same colors for their letters after one year. In a control group of nonsynesthetes (who'd been asked to assign colors to letters), only 37 percent identified the same colors after just one week.

Synesthetes often see their alphabets not only in color but also in a very specific configuration. Most synesthetes I've talked to say they "see" their alphabet trails "inwardly" in their mind's eye, but many report a sense of seeing their colored letters outwardly, too. Some synesthetes report that their photisms are projected onto a kind of external screen. For others, like me, it works differently. While I see the black print of the letters on this page, I cannot help simultaneously "seeing" my own colors for the letters. This "seeing" is not easy to explain.

I might compare the experience to watching a black-and-white movie, which, in fact, shows everything in shades of gray; yet the viewer "corrects" the actual pale gray tone of a young actress's hair to blonde, her slightly darker "gray" eyes to blue. Something like this happens for me when I read black (or any color) printed words. My mind "corrects" the print color of the letters to my own colors for them. Synesthete Alice Dunder comes close to describing this sensation of still seeing one's own letter color while reading. As she wrote on the synesthesia list: "For me, the color stays, somehow hovering on the fringe of my vision inside my head. I see the printed letter with my 'outside' vision. It's separate from the 'inside' one."

It's much easier for synesthetes to "correct" printed letters to the colors of their "inside vision" if the printed text is in only one color. If, however, the printed text letters are in multiple colors that don't match those perceived by the synesthete, he or she can find it very irritating to see the letters in the "wrong" colors.

Upon hearing all the many and varied descriptions of synesthesia, back in 1883, researcher Sir Francis Galton,[1] seeming to throw up his hands in exasperation, wrote, "One of these accounts sounds more wild and lunatic than the next!" This, no doubt, captured the reactions of many scientists (and nonscientists) who listened to such descriptions. Having no way to corroborate the strange reports of synesthetes, scientists tended to dismiss them as too odd and anecdotal, coming from a source inaccessible to scientific inquiry. To his

---

[1]Galton, unhappily, is better known for promoting the unfortunate theory of eugenics; however, his insightful synesthesia research is considered valuable even by contemporary researchers.

credit, Galton continued his study of synesthesia and suspected its cause to be genetic. And these days, it looks like Galton's theory might be borne out. A 1995 study at Cambridge University indicates that the trait of synesthesia may be passed mostly from father to daughter through the father's X chromosome. This could help explain why synesthesia is so much more common in females than in males. The Cambridge study, in fact, put the ratio of synesthetic males to females at six to one! All males carry one X chromosome and one Y chromosome, and fathers always pass their one X chromosome on to their daughters. Those fathers who carry the trait of synesthesia, therefore, would *have to* pass it on to their daughters 100 percent of the time. Since fathers never pass their X chromosomes on to their sons (mothers do that), the trait of synesthesia would not be passed from father to son. Since sons get just one of their mother's two X chromosomes (all females have two X chromosomes), there is only a 50 percent chance that a mother carrying a gene for synesthesia will pass it on to her son. This theory, of course, would explain why many more women than men report synesthetic perceptions.

According to the mode of inheritance pattern described in the 1995 Cambridge study the writer would have inherited the trait from his mother. In his autobiography, *Speak, Memory,* Nabokov writes of his mother's understanding response when, as a small child, he complained that the colored letters on his alphabet blocks were "all wrong":

To my mother, though, this all seemed quite normal. The matter came up one day in my seventh year, as I was using a heap of old alphabet blocks to build a tower. I casually remarked to her that their colors were all wrong. We discovered then that some of her letters had the same tint as mine and that, besides, she was optically affected by musical notes. . . .

Nabokov's wife, Vera, was also synesthetic; like her husband, she perceived alphabet letters in color. Vera and Vladimir's son, the writer and singer Dmitri Nabokov, also experiences colored-letter and colored-music synesthesia. When Dmitri was ten years old, his father recorded his son's alphabet letter-colors in a diary. When, in his thirties, Dmitri retested himself, he found that none of his letter-colors had changed from over twenty years before.

Like his synesthetic grandmother, Dmitri is also affected optically by musical notes. He perceives musical notes and musical keys as having specific hues. As he reported in an interview, "Schubert's 'Doppelganger,' for example, evokes a different aura of coloration if transposed by half a tone." When Dmitri talks about coloration, he means it quite literally. As he says, "I don't mean here the usual sense of color often used in describing or teaching the performance of music." For Dmitri, music and its colors are one, just as alphabet letters and their colors are one, and were also one for his father and mother.

Cambridge University's Department of Experimental Psychology carried out its mode of inheritance study with six families, each having more than one member who experienced synesthesia. In addition to showing that fathers pass the trait on to their daughters 100 percent of the time, mothers to their sons 50 percent of the time, the study offered preliminary evidence of other indicators of synesthesia's genetic basis. Different forms of synesthesia were reported within families, with some members experiencing colored language, others colored music. The researchers pointed out that if synesthesia were a learned phenomenon, family members would, no doubt, "learn" the same form of synesthesia from their other family members; the daughter might learn her alphabet colors from her father, for example. However, researchers discovered that not only did synesthesia take different forms within the same family, but that even when it took the same form—colored letters, for example—the colors perceived varied greatly from one family member to another. If synesthesia were a learned phenomenon, one would expect family members to learn the colors from other family members. At this writing, Cambridge hopes for a continuation of synesthesia mode of inheritance studies with a much larger pool of families, each containing several synesthetic members. Only time will tell whether synesthesia will establish its permanent place on the human genome map.

But if it is confirmed that synesthesia has a genetic basis, just what might a gene do to cause the synesthetic perception? How might it affect brain development to produce the wonderland of "visions" that synesthetes report? Does the single gene disrupt normal infant brain maturation, as Daphne Maurer describes? Does the single gene save the cellular connections linking one sensory mode to another, as Dr. Simon Baron-Cohen describes? Dr. Baron-Cohen points out that selective cell death is part of normal infant brain development. As the brain matures, the body "kills off" the cell connections that produced the infant's synesthesia, and she or he begins to perceive the world through discrete sensory channels. Is it possible that the synesthesia gene interrupts this process, acting to preserve intact some of the synaptic bridges, and thus allowing a continuation of some degree of synesthetic perception beyond infancy?

Or does that gene act in another way, causing an anomalous pattern of neuron firing, as suggested by Peter Grossenbacher, who conducted synesthesia research at the National Institute of Mental Health. Grossenbacher theorizes that genetic influence may not act to change the brain's cellular connections, but rather to affect the pattern of communication among brain cells. This would cause synesthetes to process information in anomalous ways, with sensory input traveling a longer forward pathway, where it would reach and activate visual centers, thus causing visual information to feed into the brain's "convergence zone," where the final product or "message" is delivered.

Grossenbacher further speculates that synesthesia may be the result of a gene mutation affecting the neocortex, that most sophisticated and recently evolved part of the brain. He observes that synesthetic responses, or "concurrents," as he calls them, are most often found in perceptions of language and music, both organized systems connected to our "higher" thinking powers. While it is true that synesthetes have also been known to sense color in such "unorganized systems" as pain from headaches and toothaches and random sounds such as cars honking and doors creaking, the vast majority of experiencers report the blended sensory response to be elicited by words and/or music. Synesthetic perception may offer an evolutionary advantage of producing enhanced memory as multiple modes are activated to store information.

In fact, the involvement of the neocortex in synesthetic experience has been demonstrated in brain imaging studies done with a high-tech process called positron emission tomography (PET) scanning. In a PET scan experiment done at London's Hammersmith Hospital, a research team including Drs. Simon Baron-Cohen, John Harrison, and Eraldo Paulescu found significant differences in the cortical responses of six "colored hearing" synesthetes and six nonsynesthetes. Using the PET imaging technique, experimenters observed the path and quantity of blood flow in the brains of six nonsynesthetes and six synesthetes as a list of words was read to each of the subjects. In the six nonsynesthete subjects, scientists observed a significant increase in blood flow to the parts of their brains involved in language processing. However, in the six synesthete subjects, scientists observed this significant blood flow increase not only to parts of the brain involved in language processing, but also to parts of the cortex involved in the processing of color. This additional activity took place mainly in the posterior inferior temporal (PIT) cortex. This part of the brain is involved in complex aspects of color perception, such as discriminating one color from another or linking color to shape. The PET studies also showed activity in the cortex's occipital-parietal junctions, which are linked to areas of the brain concerned with processing color and the linking of color to shape. The results of the PET experiments show clearly that something quite different *is* taking place in the brains of colored-hearing synesthetes as they process language.

Prior to the last decade's flurry of research into synesthesia, many scientists tended to reduce the phenomenon to a pattern of learned associations, saying that, as children, synesthetes had simply been exposed to books or classroom charts that had presented the alphabet in color, and so they had internalized its letters in that same way. Other researchers, however, poked holes in this speculation by pointing out that if such were the case, why would so many more women than men have synesthesia? Surely both boy and girl students had been presented with the same colored-alphabet textbooks to use. Researchers Simon Baron-Cohen and John Harrison did a study of children's texts that present the alphabet in color and observed that their authors had gone to great lengths to avoid repeating colors, including avoiding different shades of the same hue in consecutive letters. However, the colored alphabets of many synesthetes often contain consecutive letters that are just slight variations of the same hue. Certainly, they did not learn such a subtly varied color pattern from commercial texts. Also, how could the "learned associations" theory account for the peculiar variations in synesthetes' alphabet colors: perceiving "spinach green speckles" around the edges of a "purple name," polished ebony in the letter A, or bubbles in the letter Z?

The flurry of research into synesthesia since the 1980s makes it easy to forget that for centuries, scientists dismissed synesthesia as an area that science was unable to study, since it could not depend solely on the reports of those who experienced it. In the 1960s, particularly, the behaviorist trend in psychology ruled out subjective reports as valid sources of data, asserting that only observable phenomena were appropriate for scientific inquiry. However, the "post–behaviorist" pendulum of scientific thinking has swung back in the opposite direction, now seeing a place for personal accounts in the quest for scientific understanding. And hasn't there always been a place for subjective accounts in the fields of medicine and psychology? Haven't medical doctors and certainly psychologists always considered their patients' personal, descriptive answers to the question "How do you feel?" when making their diagnoses? Medical doctors generally form a diagnosis by obtaining results both from objective medical tests *and* from listening to the patients' subjective reports of their own experience of the medical condition. If enough patients report similar experiences, doctors come to recognize a familiar pattern of symptoms that they associate with the condition described.

Even beyond the fields of medicine and psychology, so much of the bases on which we make all kinds of ordinary day-to-day decisions results from the pattern that emerges when many people describe a common experience. Such patterns range from eyewitness accounts of a crime to travelers' anecdotes of a place we are considering for vacation. If we are considering a trip to Morocco, for example, it is unlikely we will do so based solely on "hard," objective facts such as the country's land mass or the number of meters above or below sea level it is. More importantly, we want to talk to the people who have been to Morocco and listen to their personal reports of mosques, marketplaces, cafes, and sunsets over the Strait of Gibraltar. No doubt, we will use the pattern that emerges from those accounts in planning our own travel itinerary. And if a number of people report a particular view from which the sky at sunset over the shimmering Strait is an unforgettable color, we appreciate the shared experience of beauty even if we've never seen it ourselves, and even if one person describes the sky's color as fiery orange, another as crimson red, and another as burning pink.

In their article "Synesthesia: Reconciling the Subjective with the Objective," neuroscientists Harrison and Baron-Cohen point out that the phenomenon of synesthesia may lead us to some useful insights on the nature of subjective experience. They cite physiologist C. F. Sherrington's famous description of the ineffability and singular value of the subjective. Sherrington said that although scientists fully grasped the facts of how the light from a star reached the visual cortex, they had no explanation for an individual's personal experience of viewing a star. Using a striking metaphor that elucidated the limits of science's objective understanding of the universe, Sherrington said, "At this point the scheme puts its fingers to its lips and is silent."

In that silence is all the meaning, aesthetic pleasure, and wonder of viewing a star.

Personal meaning is most vividly captured, perhaps, during the hours that one is least objective, in that most subjective and mysterious of experiences, the dream. I once had a dream that my father and I were sitting together in a golden field of wheat, having one of our conversations about color, about meaning, about life. As we continued our talk, the golden wheat field glowed brighter and brighter, illuminating the words we spoke and also the very core of our connection. It's difficult to convey the intense experience those dream images captured; I only know they have remained with me undiminished in their intensity for the three-quarters of my life since I first had that dream.

And now, when I remember my very subjective experience at age four, sitting at my father's side, watching the single moving dot of light—the "nascent origin" of the phantasmagoria of TV pictures and scenes that were sometimes enhanced by a sudden flash of my colorful words—which created the lively interest that led to my child's questions that relieved my father's sadness and cemented our bond forever, I can still hear my father saying, "Patty, isn't it amazing?"

chapter three

DISCOVERING SYNESTHESIA AT THE DENTIST'S OFFICE

Into a shadowy and deep unity as vast as night and light,
perfumes, colors, and sounds answer each other.

—CHARLES BAUDELAIRE, "CORRESPONDENCES"

The waiting room of a dentist's office is not the place one expects personal epiphanies to occur. The dullness of the ambiance only exacerbates the dread of the moment the receptionist nods ominously in your direction and says, "The dentist is ready for you now!" The wait for the dentist I went to back in 1975 was always agonizingly long. My squeamish stomach would knot and my anxious eyes would dart all over the room, as my mind could focus on nothing but the coming terrors of the drill. Even the copious magazines spread fan-shaped and inviting on the table next to me offered no hope of distraction. But on that particular day, as my nervous and restless eyes combed the room futilely as if searching for an escape route, they fell upon an issue of *Psychology Today* with the cover story, "Can You Hear and Taste in Color? Synesthesia." It was the first time in the seven long years since my father had spotted the term in an obscure yellowed copy of *Yoga Digest* that I'd encountered the magic word "synesthesia." Suddenly, my wonder overcame the fear as I picked up the magazine and turned to the story, titled "Synesthesia: The Lucky People with Mixed-Up Senses." The article, written by a researcher named Lawrence Marks, gave a full description of the phenomenon, citing scientific studies of synesthesia and interviews with synesthetes, some of whom were artists and writers. I read it, wide-eyed, amazed to find that my offbeat "visions" were part of a documented pattern of perception with a history and even a place in scientific literature.

The article described synesthesia as "an 'Alice-in-Wonderland' world where information from one sensory department crosses over to another without rhyme or reason." Marks provided examples of synesthetes who saw days of the week in color, names of people in color, and, indeed, all the letters of the alphabet in color. He described one of nineteenth-century researcher Sir Francis Galton's subjects, who had reported:

Each word is a distinct whole. I have always associated the same colors with the same letters, and no amount of effort will change the color of one letter, transferring it to another. Occasionally, when uncertain how a word should be spelt, I have considered what color it ought to be and have decided in that way. I believe this has been a great help to me in spelling, both in English and in foreign languages.

The subject's description was so in line with my own everyday experience that it was a bit disconcerting to see it set in the context of an "Alice-in-Wonderland" world. I looked up from my reading for some moments to take this in. I wondered if it meant anything that *Alice in Wonderland* had always been one of my favorite books.

I went on to read the author's account of the circle of nineteenth-century French symbolist poets and their fascination with synesthesia. Marks described the black, white, red, green, and blue vowels of Arthur Rimbaud's synesthetic poem "Voyelles" ("Vowels"):

A black, E white, I red, U green, O blue: vowels
One day I will crack your nascent origins
A, hairy corset of clacking black flies . . .
E, whiteness of vapors and tents . . .

I, purples, spit blood, laughter of beautiful lips . . .
U, cycles, divine vibrations of green seas . . .

The article also referred to the colorful sounds and musical colors of Charles Baudelaire's "Artificial Paradise," in which the poet writes, "Sounds are clothed in colors and colors in music." And the "clamor of color" heard by poet Théophile Gautier is described: "My hearing was inordinately developed; I heard the sound of colors. Green, red, blue, yellow sounds came to me perfectly distinctly." It seemed that some nineteenth-century poets were so enchanted by synesthesia that those who did not naturally possess it sought to cultivate it by smoking hashish! I looked up from the article once again to reflect fully on what I'd just read. Some people had actually taken drugs to cultivate a form of perception that was part of my everyday existence? Accompanying the article were many photographs and drawings that sought to reproduce the synesthetic experience of colored language and music for its readers. I thought the pictures, clearly influenced by the "psychedelic" decade from which we were emerging back in 1975, looked more like Peter Max paintings and the dreamier forms of pop art than anything I'd ever experienced. My own colored letters, numbers, and units of time were vivid, but their style was considerably less flashy than the magazine's pictures. Still, I could see what the pictures were trying to get at. And the article's description of synesthetes' perceptions struck a clear chord with my own, putting my way of "seeing" on the map of recognized terrain of human experience.

By the time the receptionist called my name, my dental fears had been absorbed into the wonder of my new discovery. I asked the receptionist if I could take the magazine with me, and I clutched it as I walked into the inner sanctum of the dentist's chamber and even over to the dreaded Chair in a trance of excitement, feeling the vivid red color of that word all around me. As hard as it was to endure those whirling, colorless drill sounds, it was harder still to endure my swirling feelings of impatience to get out of the dentist's office and onto the subway from Manhattan to Queens, where my parents lived, so I could show the article to my father. I wished I were there already, hurrying along the tree-lined, residential streets to my family's green-shingled house, where I'd find my father, deep in thought over one of his various projects. I knew he'd stop whatever he was doing as soon as I came in, and I'd tell him about my discovery. I was in my early twenties then, and although I no longer lived with my parents, I was going to visit them that afternoon—as I often did at that age after my dental appointments—still running to the safety of Mom and Dad's after an afternoon's dental assault on the senses.

As I hurried into my parents' house, the cotton-fog of Novocain creating the sensation that my upper lip was curling back to meet the bridge of my nose whenever I tried to speak, I blurted out, "Synesthesia! Dad, remember that word, 'synesthesia'? Look at this, a whole article about it!" I pulled the magazine out of my bag and showed him the story, pointing out those passages and pictures that most closely corresponded with the experience I'd described to him. I was too excited to wait for him to read the article himself. I immediately started reading aloud about the poets and writers who'd had synesthesia and the scientific "sanction" of their unusual and colorful experiences. As I read, my father and I both became more and more elated. I felt that my perceptions were validated and my father felt his appreciation of them was as well. When we told my mother about the article, she looked baffled, saying, "Well, the alphabet is the alphabet and words are words, and I really don't see where colors come into it!" As far as she was concerned, this "synesthesia business" was just another of the many oddball ideas my father and I could spend hours discussing. My mother spent much of her time trying to rescue me from what she saw as my father's peculiar notions or his encouragement of any developing ones of my own. As the "reality anchor" of the family, my mother tried with all her might to bring us back down to earth when we seemed to be drifting too far up into the clouds.

Over the years, my father had come to live more and more in his own world of ideas. He was devoted to all ideas he deemed under-appreciated by the world, and synesthesia seemed to fit this category. Had there been more reading material available at the time, he would certainly have added synesthesia to his list. My father was always si-multaneously reading about five different books, from Tolstoy's *What Is Art?* to Thoreau's *Walden* to Emerson's *Essays* to VanAmerongen's *The Way Things Work* to health-food proponent Adele Davis's *Let's Get Well*. The last one represented his constant efforts to cure himself of a debilitating colitis he'd developed. First depression and later the colitis had caused him to retreat from being "out in the world." But his interests were wide and his mind was creative, and when he was feel-ing well enough, he was always experimenting with one or another of his various projects, which could range from the sublime to the silly. Among the sublime was a stunning dollhouse he made for me out of simple cardboard cartons and green crepe paper. The dollhouse had a working doorbell and electrical lights to teach me how electromag-netism worked.

During another period, his basement workshop was filled with perpetual motion machines he'd fashioned out of batteries, balanced wires, and weights in order to demonstrate the mechanics of this in-triguing process. Without the interference of friction, he said, things could move, unimpeded, forever! But my mother complained she got tired of stepping over and around these perpetually moving devices whenever she went down to the basement to do the family laundry. She complained even more when my father lined half her pantry shelves with the most undrinkable homemade dandelion and potato peel wine. Deciding that wine had medicinal value, my father read books about wine making. He told me he'd learned that wine could be made from anything that would ferment, even from the dandelions that grew wild on our front lawn and the potato peels that my mother threw away. For many months, my father refused to admit defeat and throw the "wine" out. It would taste better, he assured us, after it had aged for a while. Wine was supposed to age, after all, wasn't it? My mother complained the wine was taking up all her shelf space and she had no place to put her electric mixer, her cutting board, her iron. So my father built her a new set of shelves for the kitchen. Here was an aspect of my father's creativity that my mother could appreciate: From his wide reading, he'd taught himself to build things. He built bookcases for the dining room, wood paneling for the living room, a desk for my brother's room, a headboard/bookcase for my room with special compartments for my radio and stuffed animals, and bird houses for the backyard trees.

Throughout his bouts with sadness and illness, my father was always looking for the unified pattern of principles that lay beneath everything from wine making and cabinet building to perpetual motion, to the habits of birds, and life itself. The grand design of the world was there to be discovered, beneath all its chaos and heartache.

As my father and I read the article on synesthesia that day, it seemed that synesthesia itself became representative of this hidden, unified design. Color, sound, taste, and touch were no longer separate and discrete experiences, but parts of an integrated whole, whose components could sometimes translate into one another. In its description of the nineteenth-century circle of French symbolist poets, the article told how they believed those with synesthesia were actually perceiving a mystical unity that lay behind the world's fragmented surface. These artists derived inspiration from the sense fusions that synesthetes described. In his book *Bright Colors Falsely Seen*, historian Kevin Dann comments on this, saying:

In the nineteenth century, when it became widely known that some people saw color in response to sound, those who studied synesthesia recalled the writings of artists, poets and other seekers of expanded consciousness that described similar experiences. . . . [S]ynesthesia's seeming affirmation of inherent unity and wholeness is what primarily lends its attraction for the Romantic sensibility.

My father would have been fascinated to read about all the "inventions" prompted by this romantic fascination with synesthesia. Musical composer Arthur Wallace Rimington invented a keyboard that projected colors on a screen in sync with the tempo of the music it played. Some decades earlier, Erasmus Darwin (grandfather of Charles Darwin) synchronized colored lights with the notes of a harpsichord to show the color-sound correspondence he believed existed. Even as far back as the eighteenth century, French Jesuit priest Father Louis Castel, as reported in Lawrence Marks's "On Colored Hearing Synesthesia," created a color organ, explaining, "[W]e are born in music and we have only to open our ears in order to taste it. . . . One has only to open one's eyes in order to taste a music of Colors." Father Castel's color organ had been inspired by the music theory of an earlier Jesuit, Father Kircher, who wrote in his 1650 work, "Musurgia Universalis": "If at the time of a fine concert, we could see the air stirred by all the vibrations communicated to it by the voices and instruments, we should be surprised to see it filled with the liveliest and most finely blended colors."

Russian composer Aleksandr Scriabin literally wanted to fill the concert hall with the finely blended colors of music. He wrote *Prometheus: Poem of Fire* specifically for a "Rimington-style" color organ. In fact, Scriabin wanted to fill the concert hall not only with music's colors but also with music's scents: His never-finished musical composition *Mysterium* was meant to have accompanying odors that would be diffused during the performance! Scriabin was a disciple of the great turn-of-the-century mystic and founder of the theosophy movement, Madame Helena Petrovna Blavatsky, who wrote: "Sensitives connect every color with a sound," and believed that "true psychics could perceive the colors of sounds." Blavatsky designated the vibrations of musical notes as having the following colors in the "astral realm":

C—red, D—orange, E—yellow, F—green, G—blue, A—indigo, B—violet

Some ask whether Scriabin actually experienced synesthesia or was just enamored of Blavatsky's mystical philosophy. However, others note that Scriabin's devotion to expressing the colors of music must have been based on a genuine experience, which also struck a chord with Blavatsky's notion of colored astral music.

Blavatsky's own fascination with synesthesia raises an important question. Is the notion of such ethereal color–sound correspondences the same as the perceptual experiences reported by those with constitutional synesthesia? Are constitutional synesthetes visually perceiving sound vibrations beyond the normal reach of human perception? The answer is almost certainly no. A distinction must be made between those who entertain a theoretical notion of color–sound correspondence and those who literally experience it on a neurological level as part of their everyday reality.

In *Bright Colors Falsely Seen*, Kevin Dann argues that nineteenth-century philosophers, poets, and other thinkers who did not themselves experience constitutional synesthesia misinterpreted and mythologized the condition, linking it to the romantic quest for transcendent states:

To many observers, synesthetes . . . have been permitted a view of something that seems to hold more truth than their own non-synesthetic imagery. For more than a century now, these mysterious faculties have been viewed by many as a "next step" in human cognitive evolution.

Dann points out that before the nineteenth-century circle of artists took up synesthesia, the phenomenon was known only to a few researchers as a medical oddity. Poet Arthur Rimbaud had come across the term "colored hearing" by combing through medical journals for clues to some of the nonordinary states of consciousness so prized by the artists of his circle. He then expressed his fascination with synesthesia in his poems, and the phenomenon gained wider recognition.

In an interesting illustration of the interaction of art and science, Dann tells us that the year after the publication of Rimbaud's "Voyelles," no fewer than sixteen papers on synesthesia were presented at the 1889 International Conference on Physiological Psychology in France. Ironically, it was poets' great awe of synesthesia that brought scientists' greater attention to it.

At that time, medical professionals and art critics alike sometimes took extreme positions on synesthesia. Max Nordau, who viewed colored hearing as a form of pathology and detested the idea of its being the basis for a movement in the arts, wrote in his treatise "Degeneration": "To raise the confusion of the perceptions of light and sound to the rank of a principle in art, to see futurity in this principle, is to designate as progress the return from the consciousness of man to that of the oyster" (quoted in Dann).

At the other extreme were artists and "seers" who rushed to embrace the possible loftier implications of the synesthetic experience. Dann tells of Edouard Gruber, a Romanian scientist who conducted interviews with synesthetes. After interviewing a mathematician who saw numbers in color, Gruber concluded that such perceptions were "an echo of the grand mathematical structure of the universe." Swiss psychologist Theodore Flournoy called for a more objective view of colored hearing, saying that it deserved "neither excess of honor nor indignity." Flournoy neither glorified nor disparaged the phenomenon, deciding it should be viewed simply as an anomalous trait. Such a view, he felt, would best further research in the field as it would not color the subject with foregone conclusions by either pathologizing or exalting it.

In all this confusion over synesthesia as medical oddity, aesthetic sensibility, and vehicle to transcendence, it came to mean so many different things to so many different people that in 1890, the terms and definitions associated with it were standardized at the International Conference on Physiological Psychology. It was at this conference that the newly coined term "synesthesia" included colored hearing as well as other blended sensory perceptions.

To this day, researchers are making efforts to clarify and separate the different classes of synesthesia so that we can be clear about which phenomenon we are referring to. The following is an abstracted/abridged version of the four different classes of synesthesia recently set forth by Cambridge University researchers Simon Baron-Cohen and John Harrison. The text contains my own comments and additions.

Developmental synesthesia:[1] Developmental synesthesia in most cases has several characteristics: (1) It appears to have a childhood onset, in all cases before four years of age; (2) it is different to hallucination, delusion, or other psychotic phenomenon; (3) it is reported to be different to imagery arising from imagination; (4) it is not induced by drug use; (5) it is vivid; (6) it is automatic/involuntary; and (6) it is unlearned.

Metaphorical synesthesia: The artistic or linguistic device of expressing one sensory experience in terms of another. For example, poet Edgar Allan Poe describes a sight in terms of a sound when in the poem "Al Aaraaf" he writes of "the murmur of the grey twilight."

---

[1]Dr. Peter Grossenbacher also calls this "constitutional synesthesia." Historian Kevin Dann and others use the term "idiopathic synesthesia"; however, this seems the least preferable. The term "idiopathic" is defined by *Webster's Dictionary* as "a pathological condition originating in the innate constitution of a person." Medically, the term "developmental" is often used to describe "developing" pathologies. Neither I nor any of the synesthetes I have interviewed have experienced their synesthesia as a "pathology"—although if it can be accurately described as such, then it is unique in being one of the very few that virtually none of its hosts wish to be cured of! The term "constitutional synesthesia" is, therefore, the one I prefer.

Most people who use this device as a form of expression do not experience constitutional synesthesia, so its use by writers, painters, or anyone else should not assume them to be constitutional synesthetes.

Acquired synesthesia (caused by neurological dysfunction or other dramatic physical change): Acquired synesthesia can result from head injury or tumor, which can produce an experience of blended sensations in those who never experienced them before the injury. However, acquired synesthesia does not take the systematic form of such organized systems as colored alphabets, numbers, or music, but rather such unorganized forms as colored loud noises.

Acquired synesthesia may also result from blindness; people have been known to start experiencing colored sound or colored touch only after losing their sight. Also, blind people who regularly experienced one or another form of synesthesia before the onset of blindness experience stronger synesthesia after it.

In his autobiography, *And There Was Light*, Jacques Lusseyran, an organizer during the French Resistance, describes the colored-sound synesthesia he began to experience after an accident at age eight caused him to become totally blind:

At concerts, for me, the orchestra was like a painter. It flooded me with all the colors of the rainbow. If the violin came by itself, I was suddenly filled with gold and fire, and with red so bright that I could not remember having seen it on any object. When it was the oboe's turn, a clear green ran all through me, so cool that I seemed to feel the breath of night. I visited the land of music.

Sister Mary Secord, a blind nun at Regina Mundi Priory in Devon, Pennsylvania, tells me that, in her mind's eye, she still experiences color—but with texture. As a child, Sister Mary had sight in one eye and so had experienced seeing colors. As she lost more of her vision, colors began to take on textures: Chartreuse green became "sharp and jagged like broken glass," fuchsia became "powdery," and pink became "fluffy whipped cream," while red has "the texture of potter's glaze," dark blue is "soft corduroy," light blue is "soft velvet," purple is "a thick curtain of velvet," and white has "the feel of dazzling sunlight."

A very striking case of a blind synesthete is described by psychologist Raymond Wheeler. In 1920, Wheeler published *The Synaesthesia of a Blind Subject*, an account of the color-number, color-time, color-touch, and color-letter synesthesia experienced by his student and fellow researcher, Thomas Cutsforth. Cutsforth had always experienced synesthesia, even before losing his sight at age eleven. In the following passage, Cutsforth describes an example of a synesthetic experience when reading Braille:

As the tip of my fingers passed over the word, the first time, I perceived the letter "d." This perception developed as follows: at the outset, I was aware only of indefinitely grouped blunt points; these points at once became arranged, spatially, in terms of visual imagery, and at the same time, took on the poorly saturated bluish-gray of the "d"; at this juncture, the obscure tactual qualities . . . entirely vanished and the color of the letter persisted alone in consciousness as my awareness of the letter itself.

Wheeler and Cutsforth's studies of synesthesia are perhaps better known in the synesthesia research community than in the mainstream scientific community. Their studies may have important implications for the way all people, synesthete or nonsynesthete, mentally code information and construct meaning. Some conclusions of their research are discussed in Chapter Eight.

Drug-Induced Synesthesia

Psychoactive drugs such as hashish or LSD can induce synesthetic perceptions in persons who do not have them under normal conditions. However, as with acquired synesthesia, the experiences rarely have the systematic consistency of those of constitutional synesthetes. In a drug-induced synesthetic experience, for example, a loud sound might be experienced as yellow one moment, blue the next. Also, in drug-induced synesthesia, the experience generally disappears as soon as the drug wears off.

While recognizing clear differences among different classes of synesthesia, researcher Lawrence Marks nevertheless sees a clear link between constitutional synesthesia and metaphorical synesthesia. In his essay "On Colored Hearing Synesthesia," he points out that so much of poetic and even everyday language is filled with metaphors that describe one sensory mode in terms of another—for example, describing visual images in terms of sounds, as in "loud colors," or sounds in terms of tactile sensations, as in "soft music"—that it may indicate some deep, underlying connection among the different senses. Marks refers to physiologist Heinz Werner, who in 1934 wrote that any sensory stimulation "first arouses a common, synesthetic sense before differentiating into specific, modal perceptions." So, according to this view, at the heart of our experience is a single sense that, once touched by the outer world, becomes like a "magic wand" differentiating/multifaceting our single sense experience into things seen, things heard, things smelled, things tasted, and things touched. Werner's "common sense" is also reminiscent of Daphne Maurer's and David Lewkowicz's research indicating that common synesthetic sense through which babies only a few months old take in the world.

And perhaps it is this "common sense" that makes it commonplace to speak metaphorically of someone wearing "loud colors" like hot pink or "cool colors" like mint green. Song lyrics and poems are filled with such cross-modal descriptions. We understand perfectly when a person shows his "true colors," and when we hear Cyndi Lauper sing about it in her hit song "True Colors," the title's appeal is in the term's longtime familiarity. It also makes a kind of sense to us when singer-songwriter Joni Mitchell, who is also a painter, describes her work's "chiming colors" and her songs as "audio-paintings." We understand, too, when poet Hart Crane describes the "Royal Palm" tree as "that tower of whispered light"; when Edith Sitwell, an admirer of the synesthetic imagery in the poems of Baudelaire and other French symbolists, writes in her poem "Aubade" of "the creaking, empty light" and in "Dark Song" that "the fire was furry as a bear"; when contemporary poet Elizabeth Macklin writes of

> sound nestled in bright gold as if yolk-yellow . . .
> The deep dark blues have become the only music, shown

and when Japanese poet Toshimi Horiuchi writes in his poem "The Minnesota Winter":

> On the ground sounds white,
> In the sky sounds blue,
> In the cold sounds light, . . .

And consider this rhapsodic, synesthetic description of the fourteenth-century Chinese poet, Chang Yu:

> Brilliant, bright—the flowers of the season!
> Their subtle fragrance arises in the quiet.
> Others are hoping to smell them a few times, but I prefer to use my ears!
> The fragrance sends forth jewel-like songs; singing them out loud I feel such joy!
> And who says there is no fragrance in sound?
> Smelling and hearing are really the same thing.

Marks feels that the penchant for perceiving cross-sensory correspondences is common to all human minds. Along with Dr. Gail Martino, Dr. Lawrence Marks conducted a series of experiments with nonsynesthete subjects to find out to what degree they made cross-sensory correspondences between sight and sound. The results showed that they systematically matched loud sounds with bright lights and low sounds with soft lights. They also systematically matched bright colors with loud sounds and soft colors with low sounds. At a certain level, cross-sensory correspondences make sense to all people. Marks sees the experiences of constitutional synesthetes as being at the extreme end of a continuum of synesthetic experiences all human beings have.

If Marks had conducted the same experiment with constitutional synesthetes, would their matching of sound with light and sound with color have been as systematic as that of the nonsynesthetes? Although the cross-sensory correspondences of synesthetes have always been remarkably consistent, they have also been remarkably idiosyncratic. Most researchers have found it difficult to trace a recognizable pattern in synesthetes' responses. However, Marks found a pattern that correlated the pitch of the vowel sounds with the brightness of synesthetes' colors: The higher the pitch, the brighter the color. Although the actual color might vary from synesthete to synesthete (some saying A is red, others that it is yellow, and so on), Marks found that in a significant number of cases, brightness of color matched highness of pitch and darkness of color matched lowness of pitch.

Another set of experiments conducted by Drs. Martino and Marks at Yale indicated that even "individuals who do not consider themselves synesthetes show a 'weak version' of synesthesia." As reported in "Perceptual and Linguistic Interactions in Speeded Classification," a 1999 article for the journal *Perception*, experimenters asked subjects to strike a particular key on a computer keyboard in response to hearing high- and low-pitched tones through earphones. The subjects were seated inside booths containing monitors on which patches of white or black color flashed. Subjects were not instructed to attend to the flashes of color on the computer screen, but rather, only to the tones they heard through the earphones. The subjects responded more quickly when a high-pitched tone was accompanied by a simultaneous flash of a white color on the computer screen or when a low-pitched tone was accompanied by a flash of black color. In fact, when a high-pitched tone was accompanied by a flash of even just the *word* "white" on the screen or a low-pitched sound was accompanied by a flash of just the word "black," the subjects also responded more quickly to hearing respective high- and low-pitched tones. Conversely, whenever tones and colors were mismatched—that is, whenever a high-pitched tone was accompanied by a flash of black color or by the word "black" or a low-pitched tone was accompanied by a flash of white color or by the word "white"—the subjects were slower to respond to the sounds of the tones. Although in these experiments subjects were asked to pay attention *only* to the tones they heard and *not* to the flashes of color or words they saw, the flashes of color or words significantly affected their response time to the tones.

Subjects' response time was affected in the same way when they were asked to pay attention only to the flashes of color they saw and not to the tones they heard. These results would indicate that people cannot help but make an automatic connection between corresponding auditory and visual input, and Marks and Martino call this tendency a form of "weak synesthesia." While weak synesthesia differs from the "strong synesthesia" experienced by the one in two thousand persons who generate *their own* secondary sensory responses to given stimuli (words, music, or other sounds, for example, evoking idiosyncratic colors or shapes), both strong and weak forms of synesthesia may share certain common neural underpinnings. That people consistently perceive correspondences between auditory and visual input has led Marks and Martino to postulate their "semantic coding hypothesis." When a person perceives synesthetically corresponding stimuli (or stimuli of comparable vibratory levels, such as a high-pitched sound and a flash of white color), this sensory experience is recorded linguistically/abstractly in the brain, so that even the words "black" and "white" or "good" and "bad" may be enough to generate a sense of correspondence between different modes of sensory input.

To this extent, Marks suggests that human minds are inherently synesthetic. In his essay entitled "On Colored Hearing Synesthesia," he writes:

It does not matter whether one considers perception by synesthetes or non-synesthetes [more recently termed "strong synesthetes" or "weak synesthetes"]; in both cases, the correlations between dimensions of visual and auditory experience are nearly identical. . . . [A]ll theories of synesthesia are theories of mediation. Sensations or sensory dimensions linked to one another must be linked by something.

Marks writes that modern multimedia presentations and art fusion experiments are further expressions of cross-sensory associations. From 1950s beat poetry read to the rhythm of bongo drums to Martha Graham's "danced poetry" to Broadway musical theater to the psychedelic "Joshua Light Show" of the 1970s to choreographer Mark Morris's collaboration with the New York City Opera and Royal Opera Covent Garden of the 1980s and 1990s, multimedia performances can be viewed as the quest to give audiences an expanded sensory experience. Even the pop-culture movie *Fantasia* attempted to let audiences "see the music" and "hear the colors."

In a sense, most art fusion experiments capture the difference between strong and weak synesthesia that Marks and Martino emphasize. While weak synesthesia is characterized by perceiving *correspondences between two different mediums*, strong synesthesia is characterized by *a direct sense perception in one of the senses induced by the activation of another one of the senses*, causing the experiencer of strong synesthesia to have a fused, but singular, perception. As Marks writes in "Synesthesia: Strong and Weak," "Where strong synesthesia expresses itself in perceptual experience proper, weak synesthesia is most clearly evident in cross-modal and metaphorical language and in cross-modal matching." Marks and Martino feel that further study is needed to determine whether strong synesthesia may also be mediated by semantic codes or by other mechanisms.

Little did I know, as I sat in the waiting room of the dentist's office back in 1975, reading the epiphany-inspiring article, that I would meet its author, Dr. Lawrence Marks, in person some twenty years later in the New York loft of synesthetic artist Carol Steen. In 1997, Steen hosted a gathering of synesthetes and scientists from Yale, Rutgers, the University of Vermont, and the National Institutes of Health as part of the newly developing American Synesthesia Association. As we talked, surrounded by Steen's paintings and sculptures of her synesthetic imagery, I pulled the 1975 issue of *Psychology Today* out of my bag and presented it to Dr. Marks for his autograph. "I saved your article all these years," I told him. "I never imagined you would sign it for me one day."

Just as the beauty poets saw in synesthesia led scientists to explore it further, so it was synesthesia's beauty that had led me to this meeting of scientists. This beauty was not just in my own experience of synesthesia, but in the place it held in the special world I shared with my father.

chapter four

FINDING A FRIEND:
CAROL STEEN, SYNESTHETIC ARTIST

In life, so much depends on the question, "Do you see what I see?"

Carol and I sit and drink Bancha tea in her downtown Manhattan loft, arguing about the color of the letter L. Although we disagree on the colors of many letters, her insistence that L is black with blue highlights seems particularly absurd to me because it is so diametrically opposed to the way I see it. "Black with blue highlights is the color of Veronica's hair in the *Archie* comics," I tell her. "But it's *not* the color of L. Clearly, L could only be the palest, most delicate shade of yellow."

"Clearly," retorts Carol, "Your L needs vitamins."

And clearly, something in all of us human beings wants the particular way that we "color" the world to prevail. My banter with Carol about the color of L seems an offbeat parable of this human tendency.

Carol is one of my two treasured synesthetic friends. Dr. Simon Baron-Cohen put us in touch after realizing that the two lone New York synesthetes who'd contacted him both lived in what is roughly referred to as Manhattan's "downtown." Carol and I alternately bicker and giggle when we're together because it's such a relief to meet someone who can say, "Yes, I see what you see even if you see it in the wrong color." (See pages 84–85.)

In Carol's cavernous Noho area loft, where the bickering and giggling take place, her own synesthetic vision certainly prevails. The sculptures and paintings that fill the loft space incorporate the various shapes and splotches of color she sees when hearing sounds or feeling sensations. A cluster of small bronze sculptures spiraling majestically upward incorporates shapes evoked by listening to sounds or music. One sculpture, called *Cyto*, is dedicated to neurologist and synesthesia specialist Dr. Richard Cytowic. Carol says that Dr. Cytowic "gave me my freedom" in helping her to understand synesthetic experiences. *Cyto* is patinated with the colors evoked by Dr. Cytowic's last name, mostly cerulean blue. (See page 86.)

Like me, Carol perceives colored letters, but unlike me, she also perceives colored sensations. During a series of acupuncture treatments, for example, she experienced the stabbing sensations of the needles in different pressure points as vivid colorful geometric shapes. The series of treatments inspired a series of paintings for a Soho gallery exhibition called "Shapes Seen." In describing the acupuncture source of the image in a painting called *Vision*, Carol says:

Lying there, I watched the black background become pierced by a bright red color that began to form in the middle of the rich, velvet blackness. The red began as a small dot of color and grew quite large rather quickly, chasing away a lot of the blackness. I saw in the midst of the red color these green shapes appear and move around the red and black fields.[1]

As I sit sipping my tea, I look closely at some of the "acupuncture paintings" that now hang on Carol's walls. Although I don't experience colored-touch synesthesia, something about the images in those paintings—vivid shapes bursting out of the dark background of the canvas—is somehow familiar to me. They remind me of some of the word-designs I saw as a child. They remind me of the shadowy shapes

---

[1] Steen wrote of this experience in an article entitled "Visions Shared: A First Hand Look into Synesthesia and Art," *Leonardo Journal*, MIT Press (June 2001).

running through my mind when I listen to music. The painting titled *Green Commas*, or *December 14* (the day Carol experienced the particular color-sensation it represents), seems especially evocative with its chartreuse green staccato, curled shapes. The shapes remind me of those I see when I hear violinists make short movements against their violin strings with the upper parts of their bows. I wonder at the fact that the same synesthetic image could appear in the minds of two different synesthetes, at either the touch of the acupuncturist's needle or the sound of the violinist's bow. (See page 87.)

Music-induced images are vague in my mind, but this painting has made them clearer. I feel that Carol has articulated something about our "internal landscape," brought it forth, held it up to the light. I wonder if nonsynesthetes, too, sometimes experience those fleeting, shadowy shapes suggested by sound or sensation, images so gauzelike and ephemeral that it's easy to lose awareness of their presence.

Carol recalls that the image in the *Green Commas* painting appeared during a session when the acupuncture treatment left her feeling very peaceful. The feeling of the needles in the pressure points became a glowing blue sphere with bright green crescents "raining" from it. "The image was so beautiful," says Carol, "that I had tears in my eyes when the needles were removed and it went away."

Carol Steen is not the only synesthete to report seeing colored sensations in response to acupuncture. In one case, electroacupuncturist David Mayor, from Hertfordshire, England, treated a synesthetic patient by adjusting the frequency for treatment based on the patient's report of her preferred colors: "a gray-blue line surrounded by burgundy, fading to a pale fuzziness."

Similarly, colored sensations have been useful to Carol, not only aesthetically, but diagnostically. She once diagnosed her need for a root canal when she felt "an orange pain" in her back molar tooth. "Orange is the color of a serious pain, but blue pain is not worrisome," Carol notes. "At first, my dentist told me there was nothing wrong with my tooth, but I told him I was sure there was because the pain in the tooth felt orange. He took an X ray just to humor me, and was amazed to find that the nerve in the tooth was not dead, but dying— and that the tooth did, in fact, need a root canal."

Colored pain also alerted her to the severity of a knee injury she suffered in the summer of 1998. While on vacation in British Columbia, she and her husband were standing on some enormous rocks on the beach, looking out at the sea, when Carol's foot suddenly slipped. "When I screamed, I saw orange rocks, orange air, orange husband; the sound of my scream was the same color orange as the pain I was feeling from the injury. It all blended together so that even now I'm not sure whether the scream or the pain was the origin of that orange."

"Perhaps the scream was the sound of the pain and the orange was the color of it?" I offer.

"It all happened so fast," says Carol. "It was like photographer's gel tinting an entire landscape scene."

Colored sensations also helped her in guiding the physical therapist who treated her for the knee injury. "Whenever the therapist worked me a little too hard, I'd tell her, 'We'd better stop now because the pain is turning orange.'"

Why would a person experience colored pain? What might be occurring in the brain to cause such a reaction? Recalling Peter Grossenbacher's feedback theory, we may consider this explanation. The sensation of pain is created in a part of the brain called the somatosensory cortex, located in a "valley" beneath the central fissure, which divides the brain's front and back. The activation of pain receptors in the somatosensory cortex could set in motion a neural current that, in taking its path, touches on lower-level visual areas as well. While the level of stimulation to those areas may be too low to trigger a full-blown sensation in most people, it may be enough to trigger one in synesthetes whose lower-level visual areas (like area V4, which processes the perception of shape and color) may be hypersensitive to the stimulus. Certainly, the phenomenon of "colored pain" is one that requires further study. And further study demands that more synesthetes talk as openly about their experiences as Carol does.

One of the things that struck me upon first meeting Carol was the difference in our attitudes toward our synesthesia. While I've often felt the need to apologize and make jokes about "seeing" colored words—just to prove I'm not crazy—Carol is never self-effacing about her synesthesia but rather sees it as a great enhancement. Speaking in a tone of quiet authority, her large green-blue eyes full of seriousness, she says, "The point of synesthesia is not, 'Oh, you have this weird thing.' The point is you have this extra consciousness and you use it." In her artwork, she explores the question of synesthesia's usefulness; in a series of paintings that hang in her loft, some of the streaks of color suggest the shapes of tools: a knife, a rolling pin, an artist's caliper.

Although she is committed to expressing them now, Carol spent most of her life keeping silent about her synesthetic perceptions, as many synesthetes do. She remembers at the age of seven mentioning to a classmate on their way to school that the letter A was "such a pretty pink." "You're weird!" the classmate exclaimed. (Of course, I must add here that I, too, think it's weird to say the letter A is pink—it's clearly orange.)

Carol's father had a very different response to her colored letters. Seated at the family dinner table one night, Carol asserted, "The number 5 is yellow," to which her father countered, "No, it's yellow-ochre." It was the first time Carol learned that her father, too, had synesthetic perceptions. "My father didn't mention his synesthesia to me again for years after that," said Carol. "He has synesthesia and always had it, but taught himself not to talk about it."

While synesthetes often encounter a certain resistance to their unusual sensory perceptions, they often, as mentioned earlier, resist each other's differences in perceiving colors, shapes, and other synesthetic responses. As Ursula Pritchard, a writer on the Internet synesthesia list, put it, "[L]etters or messages written in different colored letters [from my own] are somehow 'wrong' and seem to make me angry or edgy." Even nineteenth-century researcher Sir Francis Galton noted this in his book *Inquiries into the Human Faculty*. Galton describes telling one synesthete about the perceptions of another, assuming the description would inspire a delighted sense of identification. But to Galton's surprise, he discovered that

when the account of one seer is submitted to another seer, who is sure to see the colors in a different way, the latter is scandalised and almost angry at the heresy of the former. I submitted Dr. Key's account to a lady [synesthete]. . . . She could not comprehend his account at all, his colors were so entirely different to those that she herself saw. . . .

To understand this strong reaction (what might even seem like an overreaction to some), it is important to understand that to a synesthete, the color of a letter is as intrinsic a part of it as is its shape. To me, a red O seems as peculiar and wrong as the notion of a triangular O. An O is circular! And it is white! Generally speaking, for synesthetes, the colors of alphabet letters are as unchangeable as the letters' shapes are—with, however, a few exceptions. My T is a darker blue if it stands next to a brown letter such as U, as it does in "Tuesday." T is lighter when standing next to yellow-orange H, as it does in "Thursday." Carol tells me that her letter H, a flat black, can become metallic when it's standing next to the letters O (white) and D (gray).

As she says this, my eyes fall upon the glint of her bronze sculptures, and I think how interesting it is to see pieces of a person's perceptions in his or her artwork. There is a mysterious way in which a person's art pulls all the loose strands of his or her life into a new and never-before-seen pattern. Synesthetic art, perhaps, takes this even one step further by pulling in not only visual strands but also auditory and tactile ones made visible.

Carol says, "My work is about that essential mystery that connects things. At the heart of that connection is color and rhythm." Commenting on the positive influence of synesthesia on her artwork, Carol's sculptor-husband Carter once told me, "I'm working on getting it myself."

Since 1993, Carol Steen's artwork and descriptions of her synesthetic perceptions have been described in articles in a variety of publications, including the *New York Times, New Scientist, Discover* magazine, and *The Smithsonian*. Her work can also be viewed on MIT's synesthesia Web site. She has talked about it on radio interviews and television programs such as CNN's *Future Watch*, Australia's *60 Minutes*, a Discovery Channel program called *Beyond the Human Senses*, and a special BBC-produced program on synesthesia titled *Orange Sherbet Kisses.* "I was so pleased with that first BBC program," says Carol. "It was a real attempt at a serious treatment of synesthesia. It was a validation of my vision and my art."

One thing Carol and I can agree on is that to be a synesthete is to know the absence of validation. Unfortunately, synesthetes become very accustomed to traveling through life with their perceptions uncorroborated by the world at large, a part of reality not passing the usual "test." At some point we learn that most people do not see what we see and that our perceptions are considered, at best, "imaginative," at worst, "looney" or even suspect. Much of the world does not see what we see and is not convinced that we see it ourselves.

Since meeting Dr. Cytowic, Carol has gotten in touch with other synesthetes and has felt the relief of hearing stories that mirror her own. "It's been delightful," she says. "And a lot less lonely." She remembers first hearing Dr. Cytowic on a radio broadcast back in 1993. She was working with a group of artists at a sculpture studio in Manhattan. The sculptor next to Carol, who was listening to his Sony walkman, suddenly burst out, "Carol, you've got to hear this! A scientist on the radio is talking about the same thing you were telling us about—you know, people who hear things in color." The sculptor transferred his headset to Carol, who listened as Dr. Cytowic described people for whom numbers and letters had color, even people for whom tastes had shapes. Carol says, "By the time the broadcast had ended, the entire studio had gathered around me." She felt encouraged to try to reach Dr. Cytowic. She did so only to face the doubt of the radio station staffer who answered the phone.

"I have synesthesia," Carol told her.

"That's impossible," the staffer replied curtly. "Synesthesia is extremely rare." Carol persisted. Finally, her phone number was passed on to Dr. Cytowic, who called her a few weeks later. When she finally heard Dr. Cytowic's voice on the telephone, she burst into tears.

"I don't know why I'm crying," she kept saying to him.

"It's a catharsis," he told her.

In life, so much depends on the question, "Do you see what I see?," that most basic of queries that binds human beings socially. So much rests on how that question is answered in our lives: a great range of things, from how sane we are perceived to be to who our significant others will be—lifelong friends, allies at the office, spouses. People generally take for granted that most others in the world see what they see; however, for a person with synesthesia, the matter is not as straightforward.

It's not only colored letters that create the bond between Carol and me. It's a lifetime of feeling some unexplainable gap between our perceptions and those of the rest of the world. It's the experience of having a minority perception that gets no validation from the world at large. It's the intense need this can create to express that vision of the world and connect with others who see it, or who are willing to look at it.

As for Carol's R, A, B, D, and all the rest of her differently colored letters that seem wrong to me? Even that strange L that she claims is black with blue highlights? Well, I've decided that the world is big enough to accommodate our differently colored lexicons. And I believe Carol has decided the same thing, although she may always have serious doubts about my platinum blonde L. Our mutual acceptance has led the two of us to concede that the world is stranger than we ever wanted to think it was, but also bigger and wider than either of us could have apprehended on our own.

chapter five

EVERYTHING FIGHTS FOR ITS SURVIVAL— EVEN A PERCEPTION

It will be seen in the end how greatly metaphysicians and psychologists may err, who assume their own mental operations, instincts and axioms to be identical with the rest of mankind instead of being special to themselves.

—SIR FRANCIS GALTON, *INQUIRIES INTO THE HUMAN FACULTY*

"So," said Zina, the philosophy professor, raising her eyebrows skeptically, "in all my years of reading and research, I'm afraid I've never heard of this thing called synesthesia. You see letters in color? How can you concentrate on what you're reading when all those colors are in your way?"

A note of doubt and even impatience colored her voice as she queried me.

"I've always experienced letters as having color," I said. "It's not in any way distracting to me when I read. It's just the way it's always been for me."

Zina and I were drinking coffee in her Greenwich Village apartment along with Inez, the mutual friend who'd just introduced us. Inez and I had stopped at Zina's on our way to a gallery exhibition in Soho where some of Inez's paintings were being shown. As a painter, Inez was greatly interested in expressions of color. As soon as she'd learned about my colored-language synesthesia, she wanted to know more, and had assumed it would interest her friend Zina just as much. Instead, the whole notion of synesthesia aroused Zina's skepticism and even sarcasm.

"Well, so I suppose you synesthetes can have your own private code," Zina said. "You can just write things in your letter colors alone and can have all sorts of secret communications. That must be lots of fun!"

While a part of me wanted to explain to Zina that synesthetes could not have a shared color code because each perceived the letter colors differently, another more shy and embarrassed part of me wanted simply to escape her sarcasm and change the subject. Unless people are open to hearing about synesthesia, I feel reluctant to discuss it. Embarrassment creeps over me as I describe my "strange" perceptions to people who are wondering if I'm a lunatic or a liar. Although I reminded myself that I had to learn to deal with all kinds of reactions to synesthesia, my impulse to escape the subject and move to a new one prevailed. I found myself turning my attention to Zina's collection of wall-hangings, asking, "Where did you get those beautiful embroidered silks?" Inez, however, would not let the topic drop, saying, "But Pat, you have to tell us more about what you experience. I think it's fascinating that some people hear words in color, and when they want to spell, see the letters in color. And you also told me that some people hear music in color—what an amazing experience that must be!"

Seated at the table between Inez and Zina, I felt very literally in the middle of the two polar attitudes that, both throughout my personal life and synesthesia's history, the phenomenon has aroused: fascination at one end and disdain at the other. Disdain can be expressed even by educated people who are either not informed or, once informed, feel uncomfortable with a topic if it does not fit into their own perception or concept of reality. It is certainly not uncommon for synesthetes and those who study them to meet with resistance to their research. In the opening remarks to a book of academic essays titled *Synesthaesia: Classic and Contemporary Readings*, neuroscientists Simon Baron-Cohen and John Harrison of Cambridge University describe the resistant attitude some of their neuroscientist colleagues have shown toward synesthesia:

> It . . . amuses us somewhat that sections of the scientific community have been at times resistant to the genuineness of synesthesia, and especially to the idea that altered brain wiring might cause an individual to live in a qualitatively different perceptual world, where every sound is a color. To us, synaesthesia has always been an empirical issue, and we take this opportunity to thank those scientists who have been open-minded enough to look at this phenomenon in an unprejudiced and balanced way. . . . [D]ifferent kinds of perception should not be scientifically controversial, since . . . [it] has also long been known [for example] that different species of animal have different kinds of perceptual experience . . . and that genes can produce altered perception within humans (colour blindness being the paradigm case).

Recent research by Henry Kennedy and Pascal Barone of the national science institute of France, INSERM, indicates that the brains of kittens show synesthetic responses when they are in their mothers' wombs, and also during the first ten days after they are born. In addition, the macaque monkey has shown a synesthetic response. It is only now that such studies are receiving new attention. Unfortunately, science's decades of near silence on synesthesia have created an information vacuum that has contributed to misunderstanding and doubt as to the validity of the phenomenon. Some researchers have rejected the validity of synesthesia without having studied its documented history in medical literature—simply because the phenomenon "sounds" too unusual to them. Dr. Richard Cytowic's 1993 groundbreaking book on synesthesia, *The Man Who Tasted Shapes*, thawed science's decades of frozen silence on the subject. Like Drs. Baron-Cohen and Harrison, Dr. Cytowic met with skepticism from colleagues upon first undertaking his research. In his book, Cytowic tells of the ignorance of and puzzling resistance to synesthesia among some of his fellow medical residents:

I would have assumed that the charming strangeness of synesthesia and the peculiar visual conditions I had uncovered would have made knowledge of their existence more common. After all, neurology is full of strange, unexpected . . . clinical facts. Yet I found just the opposite. . . . Synesthesia's respectable two hundred year history in the annals of medicine and psychology had been virtually forgotten. Even odder, I thought, was the hostility and doubt it evoked in those to whom I had mentioned it so far. I sensed from their vehement over reaction to these subjective experiences that my fellow residents somehow felt threatened. . . . The authoritarian message that "we are the experts and know how things are supposed to be" seemed pretty arrogant, akin to claiming a crystal ball through which the faculty always had an answer.

As history teaches us, in examples ranging from perceptions of different races to different sexes to different cultures, educated people can be as vulnerable to letting personal prejudices color their views as anyone can. It is only in recent years, thanks to increased education and awareness, that we've come to have a better understanding and appreciation of the many diverse cultural differences among people. In a similar vein, we've become more aware of the many differences in learning styles among individuals who share a space as small as a single classroom. Thanks to researchers such as Dr. Rebecca Oxford of the University of Maryland, we know that individuals vary in their learning styles, with some having to *see* the new information in order to grasp it, while others have to *hear* it, and still others *move* with it in a kinetic/tactile hands-on sort of way. Just as anthropological and educational research has promoted our understanding of the variety of ways people process and interpret information from the external world, so researchers in neuroscience have been doing much to introduce us to the variety of forms of mental processing that have evolved on this earth.

Certainly the renowned neurologist Dr. Oliver Sacks has contributed greatly to our understanding of the ways in which the varieties of neurological states affect individual perception and sense of identity. As Dr. Sacks writes in his preface to his celebrated book on this topic, *The Man Who Mistook His Wife for a Hat*:

> *The . . . essential being is very relevant to the higher reaches of neurology, and . . . psychology. . . . [T]heir depiction and study, indeed entail a new discipline, which we may call the "neurology of identity", for it deals with the neural foundations of the self . . . the very intersection of mechanism and life, the relation of physiological processes to biography.*

As Inez, Zina, and I continued to sip our coffee that day in the Greenwich Village apartment, amidst plants of many species and framed embroidered wall-hangings from many cultures, we began to compare our different mental processes. I was surprised to learn that Inez, a colorist-painter, did not often visualize color independently of actually seeing it before her. The act of looking at it, however, elicited a very powerful response, which made her want to keep looking and paint her "vision" of it. Zina said she also did not visualize images independently of looking at them very often; however, she had a photographic memory for printed pages of text. Whenever she wanted to remember a bit of information, she would simply call up that page from her memory and read it off. "But what a fantastic advantage!" I said. "You have your own private 'files' wherever you go."

"Well, I've never really thought of it as anything so special," Zina said. "It's just the way I remember things—the way it's always been for me."

"Yes, I know what you mean," I said. "Like my colored words."

Zina looked down at her coffee cup for a moment, considering my comment. "Well, Pat—I suppose my way of thinking is striking to you because you don't experience it—and yours is striking to me because I don't experience it."

"Yes," said Inez. "It seems our minds are all very different. You know, Zina," Inez continued, "when I think of your mind, I don't think there's any color there at all. Just perfectly matched 'information blocks' that interlock neatly and tightly."

Inez had intended her remark to be a compliment to Zina, but the latter received it in quite another way.

"Well, you make me sound so dull!" Zina protested. She seemed offended that her mind was perceived as having too little color.

Zina had been uncomfortable with my synesthetic perceptions because they contained too much color, which made them sound a little silly to her and even suspect. But on the other hand, she did not want her own mental processes regarded as containing too little color. After all, even the most conservative businessman wearing the grayest of suits wants a bit of color in his tie.

The conversation in Zina's apartment made me wonder about our associations with things "colorful" and "uncolorful." Just what colors our attitude toward color? Too much and we risk not being taken seriously; too little and we fear being dull. I thought about the colors of so-called serious settings: the muted grays of conference rooms, the dull beiges of courtrooms, the flat whites of laboratories. Then I thought of the bright, vivid colors of children's playrooms, of circuses, of amusement parks. What did these differently colored settings indicate about human beings and their relationship to color?

Given the examples that had come to mind, our attitude toward color, perhaps, could be measured on an attitudinal range, with "serious work/somber" colors at one extreme and "frivolous play/bold colors" at the other. Is that why men in the Western world have, for decades, been expected to attend important events in suits of dark or muted colors, while bright colors must be confined only to the narrow sliver of their ties? Women, of course, are permitted to wear a greater range of colors. In America, at least, it's often possible and even tasteful for a woman to attend a business meeting wearing a bright red or pink suit (think of the lollipop colors of some Chanel suits), but not for a man. Is "more color" feminine and "less color" masculine? Is "masculine," then, serious and "feminine" frivolous?

I wondered how our unconscious and unquestioned attitudes toward color might affect the seriousness with which the phenomenon of synesthesia was taken. While synesthesia takes many forms, some of which have no connection to color, in the most common synesthetic experiences—colored words, numbers, and music (in that order)—the perception of color is central. Has synesthesia been studied so little because the presence of so much color in the phenomenon has put it on the frivolous end of our attitudinal scale? Does color hold a power that makes us want to remove its brighter and bolder forms from such serious settings as boardrooms and lecture halls? And if so, just what power does color have?

One thing we know about color is its power to stimulate individual imagination and creativity. Why do we tend to make children's bedrooms, playrooms, and even their classrooms colorful places? And generally speaking, the younger the children, the more colorful the rooms we provide for them. Vivid color may stimulate brain development. In a study done under the direction of Henner Ertel, director of the Institute for Rational Psychology in Munich, Germany, a group of children given an IQ test in a room painted in bright colors (yellow, yellow-green, light blue, and orange) scored significantly higher than a control group (of comparable age, background, and ability) given the same test in a drably painted room (mostly white, black, and brown). The children who took the IQ test in the colorful setting scored up to twelve points higher than those examined in the more drably colored setting.

Certainly, we know that color has an effect on mood. Why are travel brochures almost unimaginable without their usual bright, vivid colors? Would they have the same power to excite and motivate us to take our trips were they in black and white? It seems that the presence of color can stir the imagination and move us to action. As Diane Ackerman writes of color's power in her wonderful book *The*

Natural History of the Senses, "Our passion for color connects us intimately to people everywhere . . . also to plants and animals. . . . Craving color, we will rise at dawn or trek long distances to see scenic lookout points, just to drink color from the fountain of the sun."

We know, too, that depriving people of color can be a punishment. Drab colors can deaden the mind and produce depression. Think of the drab tans, browns, and grays of reform schools, prisons, criminal courts, motor vehicle bureaus, and dull bureaucratic institutions of all kinds.

Bold colors, on the other hand, open the mind and stimulate the memory. Color seems to help people remember things. Why do students use colored markers in vivid yellows and pinks to highlight textbook or lecture information they need to remember for exams? Why do people circle in red important items on grocery lists or agendas? Certainly, advertisers of commercial products spend considerable time and money creating vivid, colorful images to represent their products. Images in black and white would cost a lot less. However, research in market psychology shows that color's effect on memory and behavior is so powerful that many more people will remember products and be motivated to buy them if the items themselves are presented in appealing colors or are associated with appealingly colored images.

Concerning color and memory, we also know that those with colored-word and colored-alphabet synesthesia often report being good spellers, since they "see" the words written in color with the words located in space, either outwardly or inwardly. Some synesthetes describe seeing a "screen" on which their colored perceptions are projected. Others see their synesthetic concurrents only inwardly in their mind's eye.

One of the most famous synesthete-subjects was Solomon Shereshevsky, who had such strong synesthesia that he *could not* forget anything. A. R. Luria, the Russian psychologist who spent thirty years (1930–1960) studying Shereshevsky's prodigious memory and synesthesia, wrote about it in his book *The Mind of a Mnemonist.* As

Luria writes of his subject, whom he calls "S.," "I had to admit that the capacity of his memory had no distinct limits. . . . I suggested that S. possessed a marked degree of synesthesia. . . . Every speech sound immediately summoned up for S. a striking visual image, for it had its own distinct form, color. . . ."

Shereshevsky brought his great memory capacity to the stage, where he used it to entertain fascinated audiences as a mnemonist. He could recall long strings of unrelated numbers, and would recite them backwards and forwards after hearing or seeing them only once. Key to helping him remember prodigious amounts of information was coding it in vivid images and words with multisensory dimensions. As Shereshevsky described to Luria:

Usually I experience a word's taste and weight and I don't have to make an effort to remember it—the word seems to recall itself. But it's difficult to describe . . . something oily. . . . I'm aware of a slight tickling in my left hand caused by a mass of tiny, lightweight points. When that happens, I simply remember, without having to make an attempt.

While synesthetes do not necessarily have better overall memories than nonsynesthetes, they do have a particular *way* of remembering. Within that way of remembering there is a broad range of ability for information recall. Many, however, report a keen ability to recall certain kinds of information: people's names, correct spellings of words, even phone numbers, written out in colored characters and digits. As one synesthete on the BBC program *Orange Sherbet Kisses* describes it:

I can correlate the first letter of each word with its color, so if I met someone and I learned their name—let's say it was Teresa—that's a yellow name. But if I didn't see her for a few years aned I ran into her, I could go, "Okay, I remember she has a yellow name," and then I would search my yellow letters . . . and come up with the name more easily.

Cornell University professor Geoffrey Chester also remembers both names and numbers in color. Recently retired from the faculty of the university's physics department, Professor Chester feels that perceiving numbers in color gave him a distinct advantage in mentally working out mathematical formulas. Chester reports having always "seen" numbers and equations in vivid color in his mind's eye, and also on a printed page, as his mind in some sense "corrects" the colors of numbers to his own. He remembers that when he was three years old, his sister taught him to write numbers and that they all had color right away. To this day, he cannot imagine numbers *not* having color, and he still has trouble fathoming that most other people really don't see colored numerals. For his entire life, he so took for granted the notion of everyone's seeing colored digits that he reached age sixty-two before his colleague disabused him of the idea. After inquiring one day about the colors of his daughter's numbers, she told him in no uncertain terms that numbers had no color. "But all my numbers have color!" Professor Chester protested, to which his daughter replied, "Dad, don't be crazy!" The father and daughter submitted the matter to Mrs. Chester, who pronounced her husband's colored numbers "odd, but okay," as she had heard of certain composers, such as Messiaen and Scriabin, who saw musical keys and notes in color. At Professor Chester's seventieth birthday party, his daughter had him write out a list of numbers 1 through 9 and their respective colors ("1 is dark gray, 2 is white, 3 is yellow, 4 is dark pinky-red, 5 is dark red, 6 is blue, 7 is a gorgeous brown, 8 is bright green, and 9 is charcoal gray"). She plans to take out the list at his seventy-fifth birthday celebration to check if her father's number colors are still the same. (He feels fairly certain they will be as his number colors have remained stable throughout his life thus far!)

Although Professor Chester is retired from teaching, he still works with Cornell University physics students on research projects and is currently involved in one on liquid semiconductors. He tells me the students with whom he works are often very surprised at how clearly he can remember all the steps of a detailed formula they'd been working on weeks before. "The numbers and their colors are so clear in my mind," the professor says. "Perhaps it's why I've always been able to recall equations so easily." Chester also feels that the stimulation provided by the vividly colored numbers may have aided in keeping him focused on complex formulas until he'd worked them out. He sees Schrödinger's Equation in quantum mechanics in varying shades of yellow. He explains that the equation's symbol H is yellow ochre, while its basic variable, often called Greek psi, is light yellow. "It was a great advantage for me as a child, too, in my strict elementary school in Edinburgh, Scotland, where we needed to be ready with a quick answer to our multiplication tables. I could see the numbers in vivid color which helped me to do the calculation quickly." He still remembers the beautiful colors generated by multiplying 362 × 20 (or yellow, blue, and white times white): a gorgeous brown 7, followed by a white 2, pinky-red 4, and bright white 0. Similarly, multiplying bright green 8 by bright green 8 yielded a lovely combination of shiny midrange blue (6) and dark pinky-red (4). (See page 88.)

A recent experiment at the University of Waterloo in Ontario, Canada, indicates that for colored-number synesthetes, there is no thinking about numbers without perceiving their colors. In the experiment, Professors Michael Dixon and Philip Merikle, assisted by their graduate student Daniel Smilek, found that just presenting an equation such as "5 + 2 =" was enough to evoke an experience of yellow for their subject, C., a colored-number synesthete whose synesthetic response for 7 is yellow. She did not first have to see the number 7 written out or hear it spoken in order to have her colored-number response. Rather, simply being presented with something that would induce the thought of the number, such as an arithmetical equation, was sufficient to induce the synesthetic response.

This experiment showed that it is not necessary for the inducer (in this case, the number) to appear externally (as some synesthesia researchers have thought) to elicit the color response. For synesthetes, colors and their numbers are part and parcel of the same thing, a single concept.

In my case, too, an equation such as "5 + 2 =" would be enough to evoke a green 7 in my mind's eye. And even just the colors of each numeral in the equation (in place of 5, a patch of soft purple, + in place of 2, a patch of olive green) would be enough to produce my resulting bright green 7.

A similar phenomenon occurs for C., the subject of the Canadian researchers' study. When Dixon and Merikle informally asked questions like, "What is blue plus green?," C. would quickly and effortlessly answer "orange." (For C., 4's are blue, 5's are green, and 9's are orange; thus blue + green = orange.)

In another experiment, Dixon and Merikle asked C. to identify numbers when they were printed on different-colored backgrounds. For example, they would flash a black 7 very briefly up on a computer screen that had a yellow background. Although the 7 was printed in black ink, because C. perceived it as yellow, she took much longer to identify the number than when it was set against another colored background. This again indicates that for C. and other synesthetes, a given number cannot be perceived apart from its color.

These experimental results are consistent with the experience of Professor Chester, who says he cannot conceive of numbers without their colors. Also, like Professor Chester, the subject C. found her number colors made it easy to do arithmetical calculations in her head and to remember strings of numbers like phone numbers.

Comparing Professor Chester's colored-number perceptions to my own, I was impressed by how concisely and efficiently his colored-number system operated. He has colors only for numbers 1 through 9; all other colors are a combination of those. In my case, while the colors of two-digit numbers are, for the most part, combinations of the 1 through 9 colors, there are certain irregularities: The number 1 is white, but 11 is greenish-black. The number 12 is mainly white and green, a combination of the colors for 1 and 2, but 12 also has a pinkish aura that hovers around it; also, the number 2 of each of the 20s is green, but a mint-green rather than the olive green of single-digit 2. The orange of number 9 is bright, but the 90s become a less bright orange, cast in the shadow of a certain dark blurriness that surrounds numbers over 100.

Also more efficient is Professor Chester's arrangement of numbers in space. He sees only numbers 1 through 9 on his number path, which he says goes vertically upward, with 1 at the bottom climbing to 9 at the top. I could not help but compare this with my own much more cluttered and less efficient colored-number trail, which seems to stretch on endlessly in the distance; the numbers on my upwardly curved path become smaller and smaller as I stand at the very start of the trail between a large white 1 and green 2, looking up at the very small numbers 99 and 100 far away in the distance at the end of the upwardly sloping pathway. After 100, my numbers become too small to see unless I glide up the trail to number 101. However, I can see numbers higher than 101 only by standing next to them, one at a time; the extreme upper part of the trail is too foggy to see the numbers clearly.

Although my number line operates less efficiently than Professor Chester's does, it seems to be more typical of the envisioned numerical pathways that synesthetes report. As Stanislas Dehaene, research director at the Institute of Health and Research in Paris, reports in his book *The Number Sense:*

Though a majority of people have an unconscious mental number line oriented from left to right, some have a much more vivid image of numbers. . . . [A small portion] of humanity is thoroughly convinced that numbers have color and occupy very precise locations in space. . . . One such person was given fifty colored pencils in order to couch her images of numbers on paper. On two different occasions . . . she selected almost exactly the same shades of color. For some numbers, she even felt the need to mix the hues of several pencils to better depict her exact mental image. . . . Despite their

*rarity and strangeness, number forms share many properties. . . . [T]he series
of integers is almost always represented by a continuous curve, 1 falling next
to 2, 2 next to 3, and so on. . . . In most number forms, increasing numbers
extend toward the top right. Finally, most people claim that their number
forms become increasingly fuzzy for larger numbers. This is reminiscent of
the magnitude or compression effect that characterizes animal and human
numerical behavior and limits the accuracy with which we can mentally
represent large numbers.*

Dehaene postulates that such perceptions of visualized number
lines occur because cortical areas that code for numbers, space, and
color overlap at the junction between the parietal, occipital, and temporal lobes, which Dehaene speculates is the inferior parietal cortex.
Dehaene's speculation seems borne out by results of the PET imaging study done by the Baron-Cohen team in London. The research
team found unusual activity in the cortex's parieto-occipital junction
when a list of words was read to colored-hearing synesthetes.

Colored-letter and colored-number synesthesia often go together; those who experience one often experience the other to a
more or less vivid degree. While Professor Chester's number line
works more efficiently than mine, his colored alphabet letters work
less efficiently. He reports being "a good mathematician but a bad
speller." The colors of his alphabet letters have always generally been
less bright and vivid than those of his numbers. Interestingly, when
his alphabet letters are set in the context of a mathematical equation,
they are brighter and more vivid than when they spell words. However, in studying the Greek language, his colors for each of the Greek
letters aided him in remembering vocabulary words. Sometimes the
colors matched those of the letters they resemble in the Roman
alphabet: Alpha, like his letter A, is pinky-red, although a darker version of it. However, letters whose shapes are unlike any in the Roman
alphabet also have their own distinct colors: Greek lambda is brown-
gray, delta is dark green.

In my own case, I have sometimes found that processing infor-mation by color can be a double-edged sword. I remember once being in the Czech city of Prague and getting lost on the subway, where the A line is green and the B line is orange. On my alphabet trail, A is or-ange and B is green. So I kept following A to take the orange line, but kept getting myself on the green line. When people told me I had to take the orange line to get to where I wanted to go, I kept insisting I was already on the orange line! It was not until someone said, "No, you are on the *green* A line" that I realized my mistake. And I won-dered how many other times in my life I may have gotten lost with-out realizing why.

Since color plays such a profound role in information processing, we might wonder to what extent it has been incorporated into for-malized learning systems. One example is educator Caleb Gattegno's *Silent Way*, a system of teaching foreign languages that utilizes color. While Gattegno, its creator, was not a synesthete, he did recognize the power of color as a teaching tool. His *Silent Way* method uses col-ored rods to teach students the grammatical components of foreign languages, among other linguistic features. Green rods might repre-sent noun subjects, red rods might stand for helping verbs, yellow rods for main verbs, blue rods for sentence complements. Students can tell if their sentences are structurally accurate by their color scheme. The *Silent Way* also employs a color-coding system to teach foreign language pronunciation.

Of course, formal learning systems utilizing color can have draw-backs for some synesthetes, as those systems can interfere with synes-thetes' own color-coding systems. When I was a graduate student taking courses in applied linguistics, I participated in a weekend sem-inar on the *Silent Way* as part of my training. The seminar focused on using the *Silent Way* method to teach pronunciation of the English lan-guage. In this method, sounds in the English language corresponded to squares of color on a chart. During the workshop, the instructor would point to each of the chart's differently colored squares, say their corresponding sounds, and ask the class participants to repeat each sound after him as they looked at the corresponding color square for each. He would point to the orange square and say "M-m-m!" Then he would point to the brown square and say "P-p-p!" I found myself getting very disoriented. As far as I was concerned, the squares of color on the chart and the corresponding sounds the instructor was making did not match the colors I heard at all. In my experience, the M sound wasn't orange, it was light brown. And the P sound wasn't brown, it was pale yellow. The experience was disconcerting. To a synesthete, a letter's color is as intrinsic a part of it as its shape is. Researcher Lawrence Marks highlights this aspect of synesthesia when he writes, "Synesthesia is not just something tacked on to ordinary sense perception and cognition. Rather, it is an integral part of perception and cognition." ("On Colored Hearing Synesthesia," 1997.)

At the start of the *Silent Way* seminar's lunch break, I explained to the instructor that I found it impossible to learn the system because my synesthesia aroused very different corresponding sounds for the colors on the chart. Luckily, the instructor was familiar with synesthesia and told me I could just observe the class without participating. As I turned to go, another student in the workshop caught up with me. "Hi," she said, "I'm Ann. I heard what you told the instructor—and I've been having the same problem." I was amazed. This was the first time I'd ever met another synesthete! During lunch, I learned that Ann was, outside of her graduate study, a painter and a lover of languages. She was already fluent in Italian and was learning Greek. Ann and I compared our respective alphabets and, not surprisingly, found there to be only a few similarities. Ann's A, B, and C were brick red, midnight blue, and black, respectively. Mine were dark orange, frog green, and dark blue. Toward the farther end of the alphabet trail, our O's were both white, and our U's were different shades of brown. Although synesthetes are idiosyncratic in their perception of colored numbers and letters, according to the results of an experiment conducted by Simon Baron-Cohen and reported in 1999 in the journal *Perception*, a whopping 89 percent of them agree on the colors of the letters I, O, and U. As the article reports, "[E]ight out of nine subjects reported that 'u' was in the yellow to light brown range, 'i' was in the white to pale-grey range and 'o' was white." My own colors for the vowels U, I, and O fall into just the same color ranges: My U is light brown, my I is enamel white, and my O is flat white.

But despite any differences Ann and I perceived in our colors, each of us felt we had found a kindred spirit that day. In addition to our synesthesia, there seemed to be an indefinable commonality in the way we saw things, something offbeat, hard to put a finger on, but enough to make it worth wondering how the presence of synesthesia might affect the development of one's general perception of the world. In any case, Ann and I have remained close friends for the last twenty years, despite our having lived in different states for nineteen of them.

The experience of feeling "different" with someone else can be comforting and even exhilarating as it transforms isolation into intimacy. On that fateful *Silent Way* day, Ann and I had a lively lunch, where we laughed a lot and made jokes about how *our* colors should replace the "wrong" ones up on that *Silent Way* color–sound chart. Reflecting on the seminar experience now, I feel that my resistant reaction to the "wrongly" colored chart has given me some insight into the resistant attitude some people have toward synesthesia. The truth is, during that *Silent Way* seminar I was not only disoriented and confused by the sound-color chart's different colors—I was *impatient* with them, even a bit annoyed by them. Their presence threatened what I experienced as "true" and "correct" about a significant part of my perceptual reality. Certainly, it's hard to miss seeing the parallel between my resistant reaction to those colored sounds and Zina's resistant reaction to mine. Something in us human beings wants *our* way to be *the* way.

Professor Michael Dixon feels that the study of synesthesia shows something key about the way human perception works. Our perceptions of things are viewed through a lens of the meaning we ascribe to those things. Our so-called higher-order thinking or our values—the way we think about things—influences the way we perceive the hard physical facts of the world. As Professor Dixon says:

What synesthetes do is, in some sense, something we all do. What we perceive is "colored" by the personal meaning we ascribe to it. For a given synesthete, that personal meaning may be that 7 is yellow, but this only gives us a very concrete example of ways in which any given human being may color his or her reality. This raises a very big question that goes beyond colored numbers and applies to the whole human condition.

Could it be that the blatantly subjective phenomenon of synesthesia might illuminate something about the nature of all subjective experience? It also shows how much a certain part of us wants our perception of things to be known and acknowledged, even to be *the one right* perception.

Like every other living thing on this earth, a personal perception of reality, too, will fight for its survival. And, as with every other living thing on this earth, the only way to ensure survival is by learning to coexist with others vastly different.

COMPOSER MICHAEL TORKE AND THE COLORS OF MUSICAL KEYS

If man is a being afloat in an ocean of vibrations, then all vibrations are possible. Why not a synthesis? Why not a transposition of the neurons?

—MAURICE DE FLEURY

"When I started composing *Green Symphony*," says Michael Torke, who writes music for the New York City Ballet, "there was green all around because a lot of the tones are in E-major." He clarifies: "An E-major chord is a bright powerful green because everything gravitates to the note E" (which is also green, he says, but a far less vivid green than that of an E-major chord). "In *Green Symphony*," Torke says, "I wanted to celebrate E-major, which meant celebrating green."

He tells me that another of his color pieces, *Ecstatic Orange*, was named for the predominance of orange G-sharp in its scale. As he tells me this on a late Sunday afternoon, a flaming orange sun setting over the Hudson River outside my Chelsea apartment makes a perfect backdrop to his description. In writing the ballet music, he says, he literally indicated different shades of orange in different sections of the score "to capture the orange feelings of the music." As he explains, "One part of the score is called 'burnt orange,' another 'orange sun-kissed,' and so on." The G-flats in the composition are yellow-orange. The musical composition for the three-act ballet contains other colors, too: The first act is called *Purple* (in the purple key of C), the second *Blue* (in the blue key of D-major), and the third the *Ecstatic Orange* of the work's title. "The first movement of *Ecstatic Orange* ended with this big fireball burst of orange in the back of the ballet stage. It was very dramatic, and very effective in terms of the ballet—but it was not the orange that I saw when I wrote the music." (See page 89.)

Anyone expecting that such works or words would come from the mind of a quirky eccentric would be very much on the wrong track. Torke is serious, straightforward, self-assured, and also searching. One senses that his music is manifested in a mysterious part of himself that he's always trying to grasp. Torke's musical compositions received acclaim early in his career (he was born in 1961; the color ballets were produced in 1987). His color music stirred the imagination of New York City Ballet director Peter Martins, who choreographed "color ballets" for Torke's "color music."

In his clear, confident, no-nonsense voice, Torke says that he has always heard musical keys in color from as far back as he can remember. "I started taking piano lessons when I was five years old, and I remember thinking to myself, 'Today I have to practice that blue piece.'" That "blue piece" was in the blue key of D-major—and was perhaps a very early influence for one of Torke's later color music compositions called *Bright Blue Music*. *Bright Blue Music*, along with *Green Symphony* and *Ecstatic Orange*, is among the pieces that appear on a 1992 CD called *Michael Torke's Color Music*.

And what were audience members' reactions to having color made part of their experience of music? The composer was bowled over by the overwhelmingly positive response to his pieces.

"Suddenly everybody—choreographers, conductors, critics— couldn't get enough of this color music," Torke says.

This response was not only surprising, but also worrisome. "I wondered, were people really appreciating the *music*? Or were they just charmed by the *idea* of color music? And was the idea of color distracting listeners from the music's formal complexity?" Torke became concerned that the whole notion of "color music" might turn superficial and, as he says, "gimmicky."

It struck me that in a society that often equates vivid color with frivolity, Torke's concern was understandable. Can color music be regarded as "serious" music for long? Certainly the color music experiments of Scriabin and Messiaen had often been dismissed by mainstream audiences as eccentric. And even the scholarly *Grove Dictionary of Music* takes an uncertain attitude toward color music, saying that some of its experiments "relied too much on special effects." Still, I wondered whether Torke's initial motivation for writing his color pieces came from a need to share his music's color dimension with the audience, and I ask him about this.

The impetus, Torke tells me, came more from the desire to experiment with a certain musical form for which the single colors—although perceived quite *literally* by him—also acted as metaphors for exploring different musical keys. "In writing music," he says,

you start by establishing a "room." Then you move out of that room into different musical spaces. But in writing the color music, I wondered what would happen if I just stayed in the same room and didn't leave it. I thought, what happens in life when you don't want to leave a room? When you go to a really great party, for example, you don't want to leave—you want to stay and celebrate that room. So I decided to do a composition in the "room" of E-major—which is a powerful green—and to celebrate that bright green "room" for all it was worth.

But in "celebrating green," he later wondered if he'd inadvertently placed the music into a context that limited it for his audience. "Color is so powerful for people, so finite, so *there*," Torke says. "There's a risk the color can compete with the music, distract from its complexity." The colors, he feels, should not be taken as the deeper "meaning" of the music. "My music is about emotional truths," Torke says. "The

audience doesn't need to know the colors of my music in order to appreciate it." So while the "colors" of music remain an inevitable part of
Torke's own creative process, he's no longer sure he sees a value in
sharing them with his audience.

Neurologist Dr. Richard Cytowic makes a similar point about
the French composer Olivier Messiaen, who described the colors that
inspired him in writing such pieces as *Les Couleurs de la Cité Céleste*
(The Colors of the Heavenly City) and *Chronochromie* (The Colors of
Time). Messiaen described perceiving the upper range of C-sharp
as "the color of rock crystal and citrine, the lower range, of copper
with gold highlights. D-flat is orange with stripes of pale yellow, red,
and gold, while the inversion of D-flat moves through pale green,
amethyst and black." Cytowic points out in his book *The Union of the
Senses* that "the idea has no importance to the listener. . . . Nonetheless, it permits the musical interaction and transformation to take
place as a result of that synesthetic perception."

While composer Messiaen seemed to have wanted his audience
to see the color dimension of music, many other synesthetic artists do
not make their process part of their product. Certainly, novelist
Vladimir Nabokov didn't think his audience needed to know what
his letter-colors were in order to appreciate his writing (and wouldn't
the charm of reading a novel written totally in a synesthete's colored
alphabet wear off after about a page?). Nabokov's novels, like Torke's
musical compositions, have their own levels of meaning to be ex-
plored. Yet while synesthetic colors may not be a clue to the deeper
meanings of either artist's work, they are, undeniably, a major feature
of both artists' interior landscapes and the creative processes generated there. In his autobiography, *Speak, Memory*, Nabokov describes
his inner landscape as a "veritable Eden of visual and tactile sensations." Certainly, his detailed and sensuous description of his alphabet ("*a* evokes polished ebony . . . *y* and *u* . . . I can only express [as]
brassy with an olive sheen . . . *m* is a fold of pink flannel . . . *v* . . . [is]
. . . perfectly matched with rose quartz") indicates an intense sensual/

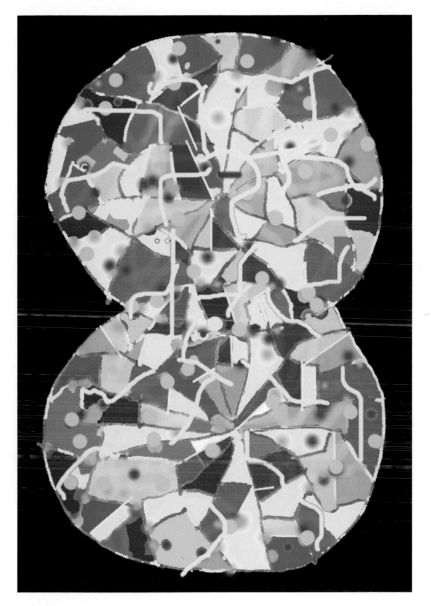

An example of a word design from the author's childhood before learning to read.

abcdefg
hijklmn
opqrstu
vwxyz

Two synesthetic colored alphabets: on the left, the author's, on the right, artist Carol Steen's.

abcdefg
hijklmn
opqrstu
vwxyz

"Cyto," by Carol J. Steen. The sculpture is dedicated to synesthesia researcher Dr. Richard Cytowic and has the patina of the colors of his last name (following the artist's colored alphabet).

"Vision," by Carol J. Steen. The image was evoked synesthetically by acupuncture needles.

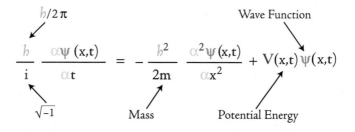

Schroedinger's wave equation as seen by physicist and synesthete professor Geoffrey Chester.

Ecstatic Orange

SCORE IN C

...squeeze the orange
and throw away the skin...

MICHAEL TORKE 1985

Excerpts from the score for "Ecstatic Orange," by New York City Ballet composer Michael Torke. The music evokes different shades of orange (noted in the score) for the synesthetic composer.

"Slime for Clouds," by Marcia Smilack. When looking at water reflections, Smilack hears colorful crescendos that tell her when to snap the photo.

Untitled, by Mark Safan. The image makes the artist hear cellos.

"Ravel's Garden with Night Glow," by David Hockney. Hockney painted with the colors he heard while listening to Ravel.

Above, colored Chinese characters from the author's Chinese language learning diary; and below, the author's name in Chinese characters, colored as she sees them.

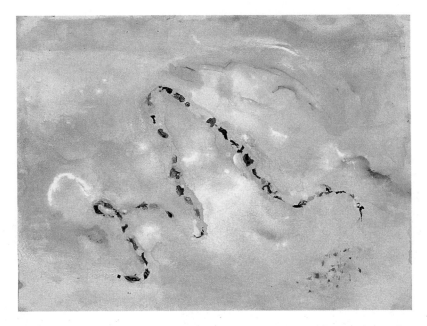

"Mist," by Laura Glenn. Glenn is not a synesthete but becomes aware of a mist clearing in her mind as she remembers an elusive word.

"Dispatching a Treasure," by Alfred Kubin. Kubin's "art of the inner landscape" is another example of a nonsynesthete using synesthetic ideas.

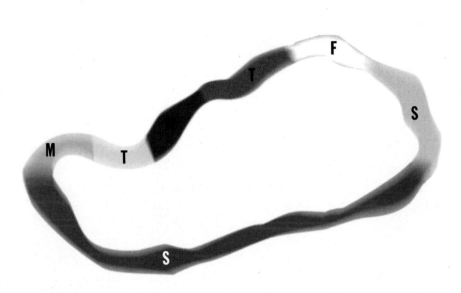

Composer Michael Torke's colored view of the days of the week and,
opposite, the author's colored year.

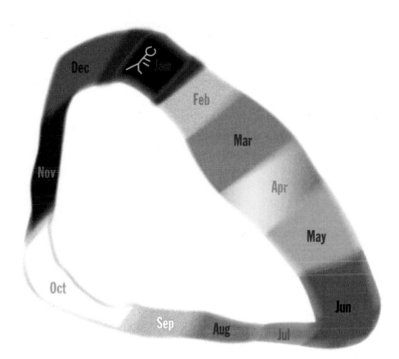

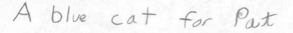

A blue cat for Pat

From
Nicky

"A Blue Cat for Pat," by Nicholas Glenn-Otis. Although not by a synesthete, this child's drawing of a blue cat has all the childlike exuberance of the author's original.

visceral connection to words, his medium of expression. Similarly, Torke's ecstatic orange, symphonic green, and bright blue music indicate an added sensual connection to music. Do the visual/aesthetic properties artists perceive in their mediums create sensual bonds to those mediums? At the same time, do those added sensory properties supply the mediums with added ways to explore them?

In speaking with Torke, it becomes clear that he perceives a visual and even tactile dimension to music so vividly that he sometimes "catches" himself assuming that his audience perceives it, too. "When I orchestrate a piece," he tells me, "besides the colors, I also make use of those dimensions of music everyone sees, like its shapes." He draws a circle in the air as he continues. "There is the round sound of a French horn, and"—pecking the air with his index finger—"the pointed sound of a trumpet, and"—rubbing his fingers together—"the cottony sound of a flute, and"—moving his fingers over an imaginary smooth surface—"the sleek sound of a clarinet, a sound like a panther's fur." I remind him that, although many would appreciate his descriptions as metaphors, most people *don't* actually perceive a French horn's sound as round, or a trumpet's as pointed, a flute's as cottony, or a clarinet's as a panther's fur. "Oh," says Torke, "I suppose I always feel they do—because I do." Then, with a laugh, he continues, "Well, maybe that's why I don't feel a need to so deliberately show my music's colors to an audience. A part of me keeps believing that the audience must be seeing them, too."

To a person with visual/musical synesthesia, such manifestations of sound as sight and texture happen automatically. But perhaps these automatic manifestations also serve a function: to create sensual links between artist and medium, while also creating multiple means of exploring those mediums. While such multiple means come unbidden to those with developmental synesthesia, many creative people *consciously* conjure them up by deliberately setting one medium in the context of another. In their book *Sparks of Genius*, the Root-Bernsteins call this conversion of one medium to another the technique of *transforming*, which sometimes works to reveal hidden dimensions and possibilities of the medium being studied.

Artist Paul Klee was not a synesthete, yet he created a visual system to explore polyphonic music. He represented musical notes of different lengths and in different relationships by drawing intersecting lines of different lengths. In so doing, Klee discovered "hidden" relationships in the visual representation that could not be found musically. He then "translated" the visual relationships he'd discovered back into intriguing musical forms.

Painter Georgia O'Keefe also employed transformational techniques in exploring her art and was moved to translate music into "something for the eye." While I've found no evidence to suggest that O'Keefe was a synesthete, her color-music paintings suggest a wish to explore music in the context of her own visual medium of color, shape, and texture, as she did in a series of "music paintings" such as her 1919 work *Music, Pink and Blue*. In a letter to a friend, O'Keefe refers to her inspiration to draw music: "I'm going to try to tell you about the music of . . . the sky tonight . . . with charcoal. . . ."

Techniques of transforming have been employed not only by artists, but also by scientists wanting to "think outside the box," approaching their complex work from fresh angles to make new discoveries. Physicist Richard Feynman was a synesthete for whom mathematical equations had color, but he also consciously practiced the technique of transforming. He very deliberately and imaginatively translated mathematical equations into sound. As the Root-Bernsteins write in *Sparks of Genius*:

[For Feynman] arithmetic progressions (1, 2, 3, 4, 5 . . .) became a steadily ascending, continuous musical scale. Geometric progressions (1, 2 , 4, 8, 16 . . .) became accelerating whoops. [Feynman] hummed, tapped and moved about, correlating ideas about the physical world with physical sensations he could perceive and manipulate.

In his review of Feynman's *Character of Physical Law*, physicist Alan Lightman wrote of how Feynman put "great value on seeking different formulations of the same physical law, even if they are exactly equivalent mathematically because different versions bring to mind different mental pictures and thus help in making discoveries" (quoted in Root-Bernstein and Root-Bernstein).

The Root-Bernsteins go on to describe how converting data from a visual form to an auditory one also allowed genetic researchers to better understand the sequence of certain genes together with their protein structures. Skidmore College researcher Phillip Ortiz transformed the visual representation of DNA into sound signals, thereby creating "DNA music." By transforming the visual DNA model into something that could be listened to rather than looked at, both the sequencing of the genes and their protein structures could be apprehended simultaneously, rather than one at a time. The reason such simultaneous apprehension is possible with an aural model—but not with a visual one—is because the ear is capable of perceiving two sound patterns at the same time, while the eye can see only one visual pattern at a time. So, it seems the ear can sometimes "see" a fuller picture than the eye can (to describe it in synesthetic terms!).

So while synesthetes experience a spontaneous "transforming" of one medium to another, creative people often employ the technique deliberately. In both cases, the new sensory properties of the "second" medium can illuminate creative possibilities of the first.

Some of the world's great scientists and artists have used transforming techniques in highly unexpected and original ways. All of us in our daily lives also regularly transform information from one medium to another to understand it more fully. Each time we give someone verbal directions for getting from one place to another and follow up by drawing a simple map, we are employing the technique of transforming. Each time we follow up a phone call with a letter or e-mail message to confirm our understanding, we are transforming. When we describe jealousy as a "green-eyed monster" or represent love with a big, red Valentine heart, we are employing the technique of transforming. Certainly, we notice commercial advertisers employing the technique of transforming in elaborate ways, not only to "teach" us about their products but also to facilitate our emotional attachment to them. In the alchemy of advertising copy, ordinary biscuit dough is transformed into a cuddly "dough boy" who smiles and chuckles when his puffy belly is poked; canned string beans morph into a "jolly green giant" with a bellowing voice that echoes over a magical land; burgers and fries are personified as an eternally cheerful clown who will also supply us with sundaes, Egg McMuffins, and even a playland full of swings and slides. For as long as we have been recording our history, human beings have transformed their range of experiences, from exploring to emoting to eating, into imaginary environments and mythical characters to facilitate sensual/emotional links to those experiences. Also, by "fleshing out" the different facets of our experience, making mini-worlds of them, we create additional ways to approach them and more deeply understand them. I've often wondered what would happen if, in the interest of public service, advertising companies lent out their best copywriters for a year or so to team up with teachers in designing educational materials. Creators of commercials have a knack for setting information in the context of imagined worlds that tend to linger in our minds (sometimes whether we want them to or not!).

Imaginary dimensions have as their building blocks colors and forms, both of which figure prominently in the experience of synesthesia. Are synesthetes more "in touch" with those parts of their brains that are the repositories of color and form, the building blocks of the mind's imagery? Is the experience of synesthesia a *conscious* experience of the mechanics and mental materials that construct mental images? In *The Man Who Tasted Shapes*, neurologist Richard Cytowic says that constitutional synesthetes are more consciously aware of the creative processes that remain unconscious in most: "I believe that synesthesia is actually a normal brain function in every one of us, but that its workings reach conscious awareness in only a handful. . . . In synesthesia, a brain process that is normally unconscious becomes bared to consciousness." And what causes this creative process to be bared to consciousness in the population's synesthetic minority? Cytowic says, "Putting it as plainly as possible, parts of the brain get disconnected from one another (as they do in release hallucinations), causing normal processes of the limbic system to be released, bared to consciousness, and experienced as synesthesia."

What makes parts of synesthetes' brains become "disconnected" from one another? Cytowic explains that a synesthete's regional brain metabolism responds very strongly to the particular stimulus to which she or he has a synesthetic response. In his view, this causes cerebral circulation to halt momentarily, "causing an effective disconnection and a release of synesthesia [from the limbic brain's hippocampus] to consciousness." Why this happens to just one in two thousand people remains a mystery, just as, Dr. Cytowic says, why only some people get migraines remains a mystery.

Unlike some other neuroscientists whose research suggests that the brain's recently evolved cortex is the "seat" of synesthesia, Cytowic indicates that activity in the earlier evolved limbic brain could be the source of the phenomenon. More specifically, activity in the limbic brain's hippocampus, which resides in the temporal lobe, triggers the synesthetic response. Cytowic writes that the function of the hippocampus is key in subjective experience. When people who are not normally synesthetic experience certain types of seizures that originate in the hippocampus, they sometimes report accompanying synesthetic perceptions while their seizures last. In his novel *Lying Awake*, Mark Saltzman describes the synesthetic experiences of a nun as she listens to a mass during a temporal lobe epilepsy seizure:

When he [the priest] began chanting Mass . . . [h]is voice was a rich sienna, the color of reassurance. . . . Sister John heard each of her Sisters' voices as if they were chanting alone: Sister Christine sounded as if her throat were lined

with mother-of-pearl, while Sister Anne's voice had more texture, like a
bowed instrument. . . . Mother Mary Joseph's voice was mostly breath,
forming a kind of white sound that helped blend the others.

Cytowic also points out that nonsynesthetes can sometimes report synesthetic experiences while under the influence of psychoactive
drugs, which are known to produce their effects by stimulating the
temporal lobes and hippocampus. Certainly, in the literature of hallu-
cinogenic drug reports, we find many accounts of sounds, smells,
and tastes suddenly taking on synesthetic dimensions of color and
shape. In his book, *Artificial Paradise*, the poet Charles Baudelaire
describes perceiving in certain music "landscapes of lace."

Cytowic drew many of his conclusions about the cause of the
synesthetic response from the study of his subject, Michael Watson,
a synesthete for whom taste had shape. Dr. Cytowic measured
Watson's cerebral brain metabolism during Watson's synesthetic
"experiencing" and inferred an increased activity in the hippocampus.
From his study of Watson and from interviews with a great number
of other synesthetes, Cytowic concluded that greater activity in their
limbic brain put those with synesthesia more in touch with the
"building blocks" of perception. Cytowic indicates that, somewhere
along the evolutionary trail, most human beings lost their capacity for
synesthetic perception except for the one in two thousand who retain
it. For this reason, Cytowic refers to synesthetes as "cognitive fossils."

I never imagined I'd have anything in common with a composer
for the New York City Ballet, but, I think, here we are, Michael Torke
and I—alike in being two "cognitive fossils." I muse over the reposi-
tory of colors and forms that release themselves from our respective
brains at the sound of music or words, and I wonder in what other
ways these may manifest in our synesthetic minds. I ask Michael
Torke a question. "If I say to you, let's meet next Tuesday, what do you
see in your mind?" Torke says he sees himself on a kind of colored trail

with a colored spot that is Tuesday. "It's kind of like a long pathway," I say, "right?"

"Yes," Torke says, "but because I'm *on* the pathway, and Tuesday is up ahead of us, a little bit in the distance—it's smaller."

"And the Friday before is back there, behind you, right?" I ask.

"Yes," Torke says, "it's back there, and the days before become smaller the farther back I look." (See page 96.)

As we describe our respective "time landscapes" to each other, Torke and I are pointing all over the place, in back of us, ahead of us, to indicate where the days are in our internal space, which is quite a vivid "environment" for us. It is the same if we talk about our hour or number "landscapes."

I remember the words of Scottish researcher Roger Watt, of the University of Stirling, who said there is a place in the brain, normally well adapted for spatial orientation, which in synesthetes is taken up with their consistently complex mental imagery. Watt observed that synesthetes often have a poor sense of direction and postulated it was because their mental imagery had blurred out their navigational skills. I tell Torke that I have a poor sense of direction and he tells me he does, too. I ask him if he can draw his week for me and he says, "Yes, but it won't really be what I experience, it won't be in perspective."

"Yes," I say. " I know what you mean—what you draw can only be a kind of aerial view."

"Yes! That's it!" he says laughing. "This is fun, I've never had a chance to talk about these things before." I smile and know exactly what he means. For a while, we sit on the sofa together like two children, drawing pictures for each other. We make pictures of respective number lines, months of the year, and days of the week. I am talking to a composer for the New York City Ballet, and although I know next to nothing about music, I know exactly what he means now as he describes his internal calendar as a trail, a meandering pathway, a *place* one goes to. What about numbers? I ask him. What do they look like? Torke draws an interesting geometric pattern that goes straight up, "but then," he says, "it makes a sharp right turn at the number 20. And I mean it's really a sharp right turn," he says, "like this"—he indicates the part of the drawing that makes the trail square off into a forty-five-degree angle, then continues slanting upward into the thousands. It strikes me how in synesthetes' internal landscapes, as in a work of art, everything has its place, although unlike a work of art, a synesthetic landscape or response cannot be changed at will. It remains as it is, forever frozen in its mysterious multisensory code. I ask Torke more about his number landscape. Do the numbers have colors? I ask. He tells me each decade of numbers has a color. The 20s are gray; the 30s are yellow; the 40s, olive green; the 50s, blue; the 60s, white; the 70s, gold; the 80s, bright green; and the 90s, orange. "Oh," I say, "my 9s and 90s are orange, too."

"Well," Torke, says, "I don't think I've ever talked about these things to anyone before, and have certainly never put them down on paper. I've so internalized them, just the way I tend to want to internalize my music's colors. But I'm thinking now, what would happen if I could show them really the way I see them internally? What would it be like," he continues with a wry smile, "to make music for an audience of synesthetes?"

Torke tells me he experiences colored vowels, too, perhaps, he speculates, because they are more "musical" than consonants. I tell him how Yale researcher Larry Marks did a study showing a correlation between vowel and musical pitch and brightness. Although synesthetes reported all different colors for their vowel sounds or musical notes, which on the face of it would indicate no objective correlation between sound and color, Marks found that the higher the pitch of the vowel or musical note, the "higher" the level of the color's brightness (although the color itself might be red for one synesthete, green for another). As I tell Torke about this, it suddenly strikes me that although many people would find our comparing the colors of numbers, calendars, and vowel sounds more than a little odd, they would consider it less odd and probably more appealing to hear about the "colors" of music. Why is that? What is it about music that makes it such a comfortable companion to visual mediums, even to being transformed into a visual medium? It feels very natural to set music to images—whether as a soundtrack to a film, play, or music video—or even as background when one watches those PBS programs on art that play Mozart and Bach in the background as they show images of the world's great paintings and sculptures. In 1999, the Microsoft company put out a Windows media player called *Visualizations*, which allows viewers to enjoy changing designs as visual representations of given pieces of music. Is there something in all of us that wants to experience sounds and images together in some perfect balance?

Music so lends itself to visual accompaniment that I wonder whether, in the absence of it, most listeners themselves don't create it in one way or another. Are most people visualizing something when they listen to music? Is music in some sense visual for almost everyone? Perhaps the notion of color music holds out the promise of that absolute, perfect linkage—even reminding us of that preverbal period of infanthood where sounds *were* colors *were* shapes *were* smells *were* tastes. What is that longing for total integration that these attempts speak to? If there is such a longing, it was also behind the nineteenth-century longing to create the *gesamtkunstwerk,* or total work of art. I ask Michael Torke his thoughts on some of the attempts to create the total work of art; of Scriabin's musical composition *Mysterium,* his piece that contained not only music's colors, but also its odors. Scriabin wanted to show there was a scented dimension to music as well as a visual one and to have his audiences experience the sensuous harmony of life through his music. Torke says he well understands the attempt at total integration, but thinks it's hard to make it work. Perhaps, however, he says that desire for the total work of art is what of late has attracted him to writing for the opera (Torke wrote music for the New York City Opera's production of *Central Park*, and his next project is writing for the new opera *House of Mirth*). But the longing to create a form of perfect integration remains.

In an article appearing in the MIT journal *Leonardo*, Torke also expresses the longing for integration when he says that his motivation to create tonal music is linked to his synesthetic associations and is "something like a yearning for God," although he tells me he's not at all religious. He identifies his "yearning," however, with the longing to find an objective truth, something against which we can measure ourselves and what we do. As an integral part of his creative process, his synesthesia is linked to the longing for that truth, for a sense of integration. In a wonderfully thoughtful article on music and synesthesia, Greta Berman, a professor at the Juilliard School, writes that the small number of synesthetic composers tended to link their color music to a longing for ultimate truth:

[M]ore often than not, these composers can be considered visionairies. . . . A common belief of theirs centers on the unity of the arts and often, by extension, all religions, nature, and the whole of humanity. (Leonardo, MIT journal.)

Torke tells me that the greatest compliment he ever received on his music was from a young woman who said, "What I like about your music is, it shows a world where everything has found the right place." And I think, in describing his greatest compliment, he is also describing the centuries of appeal of synesthesia: the promise it holds of finding a dimension where everything has its place, with each sense existing so in harmony with another that it seems to *become* the other. In the meantime, before that promise can be kept or even properly understood, we can continue fitting pieces of the sensory puzzle together. While the mystery of the total picture may not be soon solved, it can, like Michael Torke's "colored rooms," be celebrated.

chapter seven

MARCIA SMILACK'S SYNESTHETIC CAMERA PAINTINGS

*For lack of attention, a thousand forms
of loveliness elude us every day.*

—EVELYN UNDERHILL

When synesthetic photographer Marcia Smilack looks at certain shimmering reflections on the surface of the ocean, she also "sees" and "hears" a colorful crescendo of piano chords in her mind's eye and ear. Other watery reflections arouse more tactile sensations, such as feeling a curtain of satin or silk draped around her body. Smilack refers to such moments as her perceptual "Moksha," a Hindu term meaning a sudden lifting of the veil of illusion that reveals a glimpse of the wondrous. She captures the wondrous images she glimpses in ocean water reflections with the magical eye of her camera and her mind's ear: The colorful interior music she hears in her mind's ear signals the precise moment to press the shutter.

While Smilack's photographs, or "camera paintings," as she calls them, are of reflections, they are not always recognizable as such. Through her art, the reflections transform into very different scenes, reminiscent of miniature worlds, abstract paintings. A reflection of rust on the side of a painted fishing boat "taken at 12 noon when the sun hit" becomes an abstract painting-like image of *The Last Supper*, with Christ presiding over the Passover table of disciples. Sunlight playing on the reflection of a woman and her two dogs standing alongside a pier becomes *Homage to Monet,* an abstract version of what appears to be the Japanese footbridge in Monet's Garden with water lilies floating in the pond below. "The truth is," says Smilack, "I wasn't thinking about Monet at all; rather, I heard a crescendo when I saw the water reflection, which looked like a lacy rainbow."

The site of many of her "paintings by camera" is Martha's Vineyard's up-island fishing village of Menemsha, where Marcia Smilack lives. I first met Marcia when she and I each made presentations on our respective synesthetic experiences at Yale University's Pierce Laboratory. I was fascinated by the camera paintings she showed and wanted to see her in the environment where she first tapped the source of her special creativity. In Martha's Vineyard, we chat in the living room of her Menemsha cottage, surrounded by trees and a neighbor's wild turkeys roaming among them. The scene is visible through the large picture window that dominates one living room wall; the rest of the room and much of the house is filled with her "reflectionist photos" of all shapes and sizes, hung from walls, stacked on tables, propped on sofas. One large print shows an image of what looks to me like a crimson and white villa rising dreamlike out of wispy green clouds into a sapphire blue sky. "That's actually a reflection of the coast guard station," Smilack smilingly informs me. "The green clouds are really green slime that was on the surface of the ocean that day." Smilack managed to capture the image with just one snap of her camera. "When I saw the whole reflected scene shimmering in the ocean," she says, "I felt myself draped in satin—*literally.* So I knew it was a take." Smilack says she used to call herself "a photographic distortionist [because] what really interests me about my reflected images is, at what point does the distortion stop being the real thing?" (See page 90.)

It's not surprising that the study of reflected images and the "morphing" versions of reality they offer would interest an artist whose vivid synesthetic experiences can produce morphing versions of her own perceptual reality. Smilack's complex synesthetic responses are quite pleasurable to her and also quite useful as creative tools. Thanks to the reliability of her synesthetic signals, it takes just one click of the camera to achieve her stunning photographic effects—with no special technical work. "I always have my film developed at the local drugstore," she says when I ask where her darkroom is. She is often as surprised as her viewers at the intriguing works of art her camera captures. "I don't always know *why* it works," she tells me, referring to the sudden synesthetic perception that alerts her to snap the shutter. "I just know that it *does* work. I realized there were beautiful works of art floating by on the water every day and no one noticed them," she continues. "I couldn't just let them go by."

Determined to "net" those ephemeral images, fleeting as a school of glittering goldfish gliding by, she started devoting herself full-time to photographing reflections in the Menemsha waters. It had been a gradual process of spending less time at her day job writing for newspapers and teaching journalism, and more time at her play job capturing the movement of light on the ocean at Menemsha. One reflectionist photo, titled *Mountains of Menemsha*, shows an image of layered mountains miraculously rising out of blue sky. She informs me that the actual subject matter was not mountains, but reflections of the rock wall jetty at the Menemsha pier. "When I saw the reflected image of those rocks floating on the water," she tells me, "I heard colorful bagpipes. Bagpipes with their multilayered, multicolored sounds. And I clicked."

We go to the Menemsha pier where she goes fishing for reflections. She hurries excitedly along its boardwalk, pointing out reflections and commenting on their potential to transform for the camera. "A lot of photographers around here are mystified by the photographic effects I get," she tells me. "They see me here with my camera at the 'wrong' time of the day and they say, 'Oh, you've come too late, you've missed the light. You're just wasting your film, come back tomorrow.' I just smile and keep clicking." She adds, "What most people consider unworthy of attention is what I pay attention to."

Smilack's words remind me of NIH researcher Peter Grossenbacher's writings on the connection between synesthesia and attention. In his article titled "Perception and Sensory Information in Synesthetic Experience," Grossenbacher wonders if the intensity of the synesthetic response is affected by the degree of attention its hosts focus upon it. Can a synesthetic *concurrent*—such as the colorful music that Marcia Smilack hears/sees in water reflections or the colors that Michael Torke sees/hears in different musical keys or the brilliantly hued alphabet letters Nabokov saw in words—be strengthened by either focusing greater attention or a particular quality of attention on the stimulus producing it? Grossenbacher writes, "Does synesthetic experience depend on how attention is focused on the inducer? . . . An experimental study could determine whether attention to the inducer does in fact boost (or diminish) synesthetic experience."

In Grossenbacher's numerous interviews with synesthetes, many have reported that a greater synesthetic effect is obtained from their greater attention to what induces it. Grossenbacher quotes one such interviewee as saying, "Concentration will tend to intensify the sensations, while distractions will minimize them." More research is needed, Grossenbacher feels, to find out just how the role of attention figures in the experience of synesthesia. Since he suspects that it is not a different cellular structure of synesthetes' brains that produces their blended sensory experiences, but rather an anomalous pattern of neural activity, Grossenbacher asks whether synesthetes are using comparable neural structures in a different way. He suggests that certain areas of normal neural connectivity present in all human brains may be hypersensitive in those of synesthetes. So while a given sound, such as music, for example, may first stimulate the auditory cortex, it also sets in motion a neural current that, in taking its path, touches on lower-level visual areas as well. While the level of stimulation to those areas may be too low to trigger a full-blown sensation in most people, it may be enough to trigger one in synesthetes, whose lower visual areas (like area V4, which processes visual details of objects, such as shape and color) may be hypersensitive to the stimulus.

Attention may be a component of synesthetes' conscious awareness of the complex synesthetic result of such activity. If we may apply Grossenbacher's speculation that neural currents could trigger responses in certain cerebral areas hypersensitive in synesthetes to other forms of synesthesia, it may explain even major synesthetic responses like those described by Marcia Smilack. Neural currents set in motion by looking at a certain quality of light could touch hypersensitive areas of the visual and auditory cortex, producing the enchanting blended sensory effects this artist experiences. In addition, Smilack's sudden directing of highly focused attention on the synesthetic inducer—in her case, ocean reflections—could significantly strengthen the vividness of an already hypersensitive response, thus producing the blended sensory effects she describes.

Marcia Smilack's photographic work is so original and professional that it's hard to believe that she came to photography as late in life as she did. "For most of my life, I'd been a journalist," says this veteran writer for several Boston newspapers who has a Ph.D. in literature from Brown University, where she also worked as a visiting journalism professor. "Then I began working on a book about the experiences of medical personnel during the war in Vietnam. Many of the interviews I did with nurses and doctors revealed stories of experiences so horrifying," she says, "that at a certain point, I couldn't go on with the project. I'd reached my limit and didn't even want to write at all anymore, about anything. I decided I had to find a new, nonverbal means of expression. I started going to the ocean with my camera and tried to capture its floating world of light." Her synesthesia blended with the process, and, as she says, "It seemed to become even more vivid for me the more I focused on it, taking my reflection-photos."

Another striking example of the connection between synesthetic response and degree of attention is in the work of California artist Ruth Armer. For many years, Armer had been a very realistic painter of animals and birds in their natural habitats. When she became ill, she lay bed-ridden, frustrated that she could no longer go outside to paint from nature. Lying in bed, she spent much time listening to classical music and became aware that it expressed itself as colorful images in her mind's eye. The result was her series of "music paintings" of the works of Wagner, Mozart, and Schoenberg. Interestingly, Armer told of a (nonsynesthete) musician who, looking at her paintings, was able to name the composer of the musical works each represented! Armer had the sense her music images had always been there, but her attention to them had not. Before her illness, her eye had been on the external world of nature, which she observed closely and painted meticulously. But now, directing the same quality of close attention to those internal, music-induced images, she saw them clearly and vividly for the first time and began to paint them.

Mark Safan, an artist and musician for whom music evokes colors and colors in paintings evoke music, tells a similar story of suddenly gaining greater awareness of the intricacies of his internal imagery. He traces this back to sitting in his high school class, attentively watching the clock and waiting eagerly for its hands to reach 3:20 P.M., the hour of release. He became aware that the "bright yellow-orange and flame-blue" colors of 3:20 were like those of the flower called bird of paradise, an image that corresponded to his own feeling of liberation when the clock struck 3:20. During this period of his life he began making paintings and writing music and became aware of the latter's colors and the former's music: Looking at certain shades of deep red with yellow highlights in artist Mark Rothko's paintings evoked the sounds of cellos; the music of the Beatles' *Sergeant Pepper* album was "saturated with colored textures," while Stravinsky's *Rite of Spring* was full of "colored abstract forms." Safan says he frequently "hears inward melodies" as he paints. (See page 91.)

In an essay entitled "Perception and Sensory Information in Synaesthetic Experience," Peter Grossenbacher writes of how the

quality of attention may affect strength and intensity of the synesthetic response to music:

The fact that music is a common synesthetic inducer suggests that it might be
the way in which people listen to sounds that induces synesthetic experience.
Would concurrent phenomenal coloration arise if the listener were not
consciously following the melody?

The experience of contemporary American composer Jay Alan
Yim also points to the role of attention in synesthesia. The recipient
of many musical awards and creator of the celebrated piece *Rough*
Magic, performed by the Chicago Symphony Orchestra, Yim became
aware of a synesthetic response during one of his repeated drives
through New Mexico's Sandia Mountains. As the program notes to
a performance of *Rough Magic* report, when he drove through the
mountains and watched the effect of the changing light on their colors, he became aware of

an inner hearing of a massive series of dense chords, like sonic monoliths, one
always slowly succeeding the other. It was a very vivid experience and it was
repeated on a number of occasions; over time, I felt compelled to express this
musically, and I concluded that the symphony orchestra was probably the best
medium.

World-renowned painter David Hockney experiences synesthesia
when he listens to music while painting. In *The Union of the Senses*, neurologist Dr. Richard Cytowic, who interviewed Hockney, quotes the
artist as saying of his synesthetic experience, "You know, I never
thought there was anything unusual about this." Using specially pre-
pared tapes along with color chips and geometric shapes, Dr. Cytowic
had Hockney match colors and shapes to the recorded musical notes,
which the artist did with great precision, taking great pains to match

the exact shades of the hues he perceived in response to given musical notes. Cytowic finds that this insistence on preciseness of shade when matching a given sound with a color is a hallmark of those with synesthesia. As Cytowic writes, "This infinite variety of a single color, this exactness of shade, is a typical synesthetic comment."

Hockney became more aware of the complexity of his synesthetic response when he began painting stage sets for the Metropolitan Opera. As he painted and listened to the opera's music, he became aware of the complexity of color shades that "composed" it. Of the opera *Rossignol*, Hockney says, the first thing you notice about it is that "it's all blue." But as he listened again and again while painting, he became aware that the music was, as he said, "infinite varieties of blue . . . and transparent." The assorted blues took on a spatial quality. Wanting to show the shades of blue in three dimensions, Hockney used seventeenth-century Chinese blue porcelain plates as a motif for his stage set. In his interview with Hockney, Cytowic quotes the painter as saying, "I find that visual equivalents for music reveal themselves. In Ravel, certain passages seem to me all blue and green and certain shapes begin to suggest themselves almost naturally." (See page 92.)

As for the music of Stravinsky's *Oedipus Rex*, Hockney says, "there were lines and sharp things which suggested cross hatchings. . . . [T]he music is like this—horizontal and vertical, very geometric. . . . In all the operas I've done, the music gives me the set—the color and the shape." Cytowic says that Hockney's more intense synesthetic experiences led the artist to explore further "the nature of space," as he did in his three-dimensional scenery for the opera *Tristan and Isolde* and in his photo collages.

Much of our creative process is submerged below our conscious awareness. Sometimes, however, if we focus on something in a particularly intense way—even something we've experienced many times before—startling new perceptions of it can come into our conscious view. Marcia Smilack's increased capacity to attend to fleeting sea-reflected images can almost become a metaphor for the potential capacity we all have to attend more fully—and differently—to those vague "sensings" that float on the edge of our conscious awareness.

Perhaps it is the rich world of blended sensations that makes it possible for synesthetes to attend easily to their inner worlds, to sit daydreaming, reflecting, or otherwise ruminating for long periods. I've often had the sense that Smilack and other synesthetes I've met could remain contentedly in their own spaces—studios, workshops, or studies—for weeks and even months on end, wholeheartedly attending to their creative endeavors. I think of Marcia's little house in the Menemsha woods, brimming with reflectionist photos and other creative experiments; of Carol Steen's studio with her many paintings and sculptures of synesthetic sensations ranging from the feel of acupuncture needles to the sound of a wolf cry; of Professor Geoffrey Chester at Cornell University, working out his colored equations; of Michael Torke's description of the many hours he spent writing his musical score for *Ecstatic Orange* in the many shades of that color. These creative people have attended to and are increasingly in touch with their inner worlds and the particular synesthetic forms their perceptions take.

But is there ever a downside to all this? Could the inner world become so compelling that it might sometimes rival the outer for its share of attention? Smilack admits that although she would never want to lose her synesthesia, "Sometimes I have trouble getting myself out of the house." She explains, "I have so many ideas for creative projects, always capturing my attention. But sometimes my fear is," she continues, pointing to a copy of the book *The Mind of a Mnemonist* about Shereshevsky (the Russian synesthete who felt his mind so overstuffed with images that he had trouble putting them out of his conscious mind), "that I'm going to become like *him*—just all closed up in my own mind. As it is, weeks go by when I don't read the newspaper. And imagine—I used to be a *journalist*," she tells me.

Of course, just the fact that Smilack *had been* a journalist for so many years attests to her considerable capacity to focus on outer life as well as inner life. The same could be said of virtually all of the synesthetes described in this book, whose active lives and often rewarding careers indicate their capacity to draw on their rich inner worlds to contribute to the "exterior" world shared with others. Yet I wonder—do synesthetes generally have the capacity to sink more easily into, for lack of a better term, a state of "creative reverie"? Do they have a preference for activity that requires long solitary stretches of focusing on their inner thoughts and envisionings? Do the fused sensory experiences of their inner worlds provide a high enough degree of stimulation to keep their minds contentedly occupied? Judging by the synesthetes I've met—and by my own experience—I would say that boredom is not an emotion synesthetes experience very often—not as long as we are able to sink into our interior spaces. Of course, many creative people who are *not* synesthetes have this capacity, too. My father never reported having any synesthetic perceptions, yet he could remain in his basement workshop for hours, considering a new idea he'd just read, poring over his latest invention, or simply thinking up a new one. Minds come in a great variety of types, of which the synesthetic is just one. We might consider, nevertheless, what effect synesthesia has on the general state of consciousness, or whether its presence could indicate a particular quality of consciousness. Could the ability to drift more easily into states of reverie or other altered states be a marker of synesthesia? Concerning this question, Cytowic writes that synesthetes, as a group, "seem more prone to unusual experiences": déjà-vu, clairvoyance, precognitive dreams, the feeling of presences "are encountered often enough."

Dmitri Nabokov reports experiencing some extraordinary mental phenomena in his repertoire of synesthetic experience. One experience he describes is the sense of "colors on the top of my halo." He senses particular colors hovering halo-like just above his head if he has the sense that his thoughts appeal to the divine. In our interview, he said, "I do not subscribe to any religious creed, but if, at times, a segment of my conscious or subconscious appeals to a higher authority, one or two intense tints tend to color the sensation."

Although Cytowic does not regard constitutional synesthesia as pathological, he feels synesthetes share certain characteristics with those who experience temporal lobe epilepsy. The great Russian novelist Dostoyevsky, who suffered from temporal lobe epilepsy, reported experiencing colored sound and feelings of transcendence during seizures. When the temporal lobes are in a state of heightened activity, unusual mental phenomena can be experienced. Studies have shown that all people are capable of having experiences defined as hallucinatory or synesthetic if their temporal lobes are stimulated. In the 1950s, Canadian researcher Wilder Penfield showed that temporal lobe stimulation could evoke for people such powerful scenes of stored memories that they actually had the sensation of reliving those moments. Subjects in the experiments typically reported externally seeing the people and things in the relived scenes and those in present exterior reality at the same time. This is reminiscent of colored-language synesthetes who report seeing their synesthetically colored words on a page of text *and* the color of the text's print at the same time. As Dr. Cytowic writes in *The Man Who Tasted Shapes*, "Like synesthetes, patients who had a temporal lobe stimulated could appreciate 'both worlds.'" Thus, a synesthetic experience could also indicate greater temporal lobe activation.

Besides a possibly greater inclination to sink into creative reverie, are there other mental features that may be markers of synesthesia? Researchers Simon Baron-Cohen and John Harrison observed another regular feature of synesthetes' consciousness: their consistent dreaming in color. Baron-Cohen and Harrison found that, when they asked subjects, both synesthete and nonsynesthete, whether they dreamed in color, most of the nonsynesthetes answered that they sometimes dreamed in color, or never did, or that they didn't remember dreaming at all. However, *all* of the synesthetes interviewed reported dreaming in color *all* of the time.

Interestingly, in his book *An Anthropologist on Mars*, Oliver Sacks writes of a painter, Jonathan I., who, following an accident, lost his ability to dream in color, to experience colored-music synesthesia (which he had been able to do before his accident), and to perceive the colors of the external world (he could perceive them only in shades of gray). Jonathan I.'s experience may offer further indications of a neural link between color dreaming and forms of color synesthesia.

Synesthetes even have difficulty grasping the notion of *not* dreaming in color. One synesthete told me of the day her third grade teacher told the class that most people dream in black and white. Upset and confused, she ran home after school, insisting her mother tell her this was not true of anyone in their family. It was quite a rude awakening for her to learn that her mother was among the black-and-white dreamers! I myself can neither recollect nor easily imagine dreaming in black and white. The idea of things *losing* their colors in dreams seems very odd to me because in my dreams, the colors of things generally match those I see in waking life. In some dreams, however, certain colors take on a heightened quality, as they did in the dream about my father and the glowing golden wheat field (related in Chapter Three). I remember having another intensely colored dream where the turquoise ocean of Bermuda merged with an equally turquoise Bermuda sky until the two became one vast space of turquoise "oceansky" with no discernible borders between them. The turquoise color of this oceansky was far more intense than any shade of this color I've seen in waking life. Also, on rare occasions, I've experienced forms of synesthesia in my dreams that I never have in waking life. Once I dreamed of a windy forest of trees blowing music. In the dream, there was no separation between the movement of the trees and the sound of the music. It was a single, "sensorily borderless" event. If Marcia Smilack experiences the feel of satin as she looks at certain ocean reflections, I experienced the music of movement as I watched blowing trees.

Smilack, who always dreams in color, remembers one dream where her synesthetic colors for music differed from those she experiences in waking life:

I had a wonderful dream in which I was playing a harpsichord (in real life, I have never done this). This particular harpsichord had a series of overlapping squares of color laid across the top. . . . Their placement over the strings didn't interfere with my playing in the least; to the contrary, I was able to "play" the colors so well that by the end I'd discovered I could draw out an extended vibrato perfectly. It was quite a thrill. The only surprise upon wakening was the colors themselves: They were almost primary and quite dark in tone, while in real life the sounds produced by strings—at least of a harp—always make me see pastels. In the dream, the colors included red, burgundy, rusty brown, and navy blue. I don't know what this means, but I'm guessing that when the sound becomes baroque, the colors must deepen.

Smilack also says that some of the colorful images in her dreams later appear in her reflectionist photos. This was the case with the image in her "green cloud" photo (titled *Slime for Clouds*). In one such dream, she was watching the Menemsha sky at sunset when two "green-as-grass" clouds floated by, much like the ones that later appeared in her camera painting.

Synesthetes report often remembering their dreams and also using them in a helpful way in waking life. Could it be that the generally heightened activity in their temporal lobes—which also figure prominently in dreaming—causes them to attend more intently to their dreams, thus remembering them more vividly and finding their contents useful?

When we dream, we experience a strange juxtaposition of elements, which nevertheless seems to have a sensible integration and be meaningful to us. It is only upon waking that the combination of dream events often makes no sense at all (although it clearly did to some aspect of our unconscious mind). Could it be that synesthetes' integration of colors and shapes with music or language "makes sense" to them in the same way that integration of dream elements makes sense to the dreamer? And could a certain quality of attention make synesthetes more focused on the inner world of dreams and other visions?

Interestingly, French philosopher Merleau-Ponty wrote admiringly of the sensory integration indicated by synesthesia in his book *Phenomenology of Perception*. He felt that our fragmented social experience led to diminished sensory capacity, saying, "Synesthesia is the rule. . . . [W]e unlearn how to see, hear, and generally speaking, feel." Whether or not synesthetic perception is actually "the rule," we probably would agree that with greater attention, we might experience greater perceptual integration and variety than we habitually do.

A reorientation of our attention creates a reorientation to the world. In the best-selling book *Flow: The Psychology of Optimal Experience*, which explores the blissfully integrated state of consciousness produced by total absorption in a meaningful task, psychologist Mihaly Csikszentmihalyi writes, "The shape and content of life depend on how attention has been used. Entirely different realities will emerge, depending on how it is invested." Perhaps that is why the American poet William Carlos Williams always used to carry a pad of paper with the title "Things I Noticed Today that I've Missed Until Today." Keeping such a notebook was a way for Williams to cultivate, expand, and reorient his attention to both the world without and within, certainly a prerequisite for the writing of poems.

Diverse cultures have recognized the importance of developing the art of attention as a way to expand the repertoire of our experience. That is why they have developed a range of rituals and exercises, from meditation, martial arts, and Japanese tea ceremonies to Chinese garden viewing and European labyrinth walking—systems designed to focus and reorient our attention so we can see aspects of reality that may have previously eluded us. Cultivating the art of attention is also a way to gain greater insight into how our minds work. Every one of us—synesthete or nonsynesthete—has a unique blueprint of reality, a unique way of coding knowledge that is different from any other on earth. But some expressions of that code are hidden from our view, floating somewhere on the shadowy edge of conscious awareness. By quieting down the habitually "louder" parts of our mind and turning the dial of our attention to its darker, quieter places, we may hear our personal code's unique and usually unheard "song," needing the touch of our attention to turn up its volume. Perhaps the thirteenth-century Sufi poet Rumi had this kind of attending in mind when he wrote:

> *In the name of this place*
> *we drink in with our breathing, stay quiet like a flower*
> *So the night birds will start singing.*

chapter eight

PERSONAL CODING

To teach the unfamiliar, set it alongside the familiar.

—CHINESE SAYING

Walking into the train station in Shanghai for the first time in December 1986, I felt I was stepping onto another planet, so flooded was I by sights unfamiliar: throngs of men in Mao suits, peasant women laden with bags and baskets brimming with unidentifiable fruits, vegetables, and other contents, and huge signs all around written in indecipherable Chinese. I had an overwhelming sense of the impossibility of ever figuring out where I was, let alone finding the train I needed. Had I not been with my husband, Josh, who is fluent in Chinese, I might have remained in that station for days, wandering helplessly and hopelessly through a bewildering wonderland of unreadable signs and unfathomable symbols.

About ten months after that first trip and glimpse into what seemed an impenetrable world, Josh and I had an opportunity to return to China for a year, from 1987 to 1988, when I was hired to make a series of TV programs on American language and culture for the Television University of China. During that year, the Chinese language became a dominant, daily reality and also the bridge that could connect me to the life of the intriguing city of Nanjing, whose streetmarkets, throngs of bicyclers, pedestrians, and their thousands of different life stories fascinated me. I wanted to ride my bicycle to the marketplace and chat with the sellers who were generally curious about the foreigners in their midst, but had little possibility of com-municating with them. For many of them, it seemed to me, Western people were part of a remote landscape even when they were right there in the middle of the street market.

After a couple of months in China, I learned enough of the lan-guage to feel comfortable in asking directions (if I got lost riding my bicycle), shopping at the outdoor free markets, and chatting with the sellers whose questions were repeated so often ("What country are you from?," "What are you doing in China?," "Can you use chop-sticks?"). In my twice-weekly lessons in spoken Chinese, I kept a notebook of newly learned vocabulary words. I wrote the words, not in Chinese characters, but in pinyin, a system for writing Chinese words using a Roman alphabet.

In learning Chinese, I depended heavily on the pinyin system, but that was not my only aid. Because of my synesthesia, I could "see" the Chinese words spelled out in pinyin or Roman letters, in their vari-ous colors, as was standard for me in processing words in general. By using pinyin, I was operating within a very familiar system. What was different about the process, however, was the way my mind coded the language's *tones*. Unlike English, Chinese is a tonal language, which means any given syllable could have multiple pronunciations and meanings, depending on its tone or intonation. The four tones of Mandarin Chinese are (1) even, (2) rising, (3) falling-rising, and (4) falling. In my mind's eye, the colorful Chinese words sloped upward, downward, took a dip in the middle, or stayed even depending on their tones (see page 93). Since a single syllable could be one of four different words, depending upon its intonation, it's easy for foreigners learning Chinese to mix words up. For example, the word *mai* with a falling tone means "sell," but if its intonation first falls and then rises, it means "buy." Similarly, the word *tang* with a rising tone means "sugar," but *tang* with an even tone means "soup." (I'll never forget the day that a confused Chinese shopkeeper thought I wanted to sell him some soup when in fact I wanted to buy some sugar!)

Despite such errors, my synesthetic color and sloping imagery sometimes helped me to distinguish one spoken Chinese word from another. Unfortunately, this imagery was of no use in helping me learn to *read* Chinese characters. When my first year of work ended in 1988, I left China knowing quite a bit more spoken Chinese than I had when I arrived, but I could read virtually nothing.

A decade later, an opportunity came up that allowed me to visit China again. For five months in 1998, I went to join my husband, who had a job directing a translation project. During those months, as I learned to speak a bit more Chinese, it became increasingly frustrating and awkward not to know any of the written language. To avoid misunderstandings during conversations, Chinese people will often write particular characters for foreigners. But I did not know the characters they were writing for me. Sometimes, the fact that I could speak some Chinese led them to believe I could read and write some Chinese, too. They were surprised to learn that I was, in reality, almost totally illiterate. I feared I would leave China again knowing nothing of its written language.

Determined not to let that happen, about a month before my stay in China ended I had an idea. I decided to try an experiment where I would very consciously use my synesthesia as an aid to learning at least a few written Chinese words. I kept a notebook/diary where I wrote certain basic words in my colored romanized alphabet letters of pinyin (in accordance with my colored alphabet letters). Next to the colored pinyin I wrote the corresponding character in the same colors. Since all my colored words tend to take on the color cast of their first letters, I drew the Chinese character in the word's basic color, then added some touches of color from the word's other letters. The first character that I drew was *kai*, the Chinese word for "to open." *Kai* was chartreuse green (like the letter K) with touches of dark orange and white for its A and I, respectively. (In retrospect, it seems an appropriate choice to have started with a word that meant "open," since this method "opened" a way into the written Chinese language for me.) I wrote about thirty colored characters in my notebook/ diary. I also wrote little stories in pinyin about funny misunderstandings that had happened in my attempts to learn the Chinese language. Under each of the colored pinyin words in my story, my teacher would write the corresponding Chinese character, which I colored in, using colors that matched those of the pinyin words. Chinese characters are composed of several different "radicals," or what we might call morphemes, or units of meaning. For example, the character for the word "good" is a combination of the characters for the words "son" and "daughter," for if one has a son and a daughter, that's good. As I developed a little more knowledge of Chinese, I also experimented with the notion of drawing basic Chinese radicals in their particular colors and combining them to make new characters. I had a lot of fun making this notebook, which encouraged me to focus on characters, instead of resist them. Although I kept the diary only during my last month in China, even now, I never fail to recognize the Chinese characters I learned using my synesthetic colors.

Setting the remote characters into the familiar context of my synesthetic imagery made them less remote, more a part of my personal inner landscape. By giving the characters colors with familiar associations, I put them into a context that was comfortable and non-threatening. When I saw them written in colors that had emotional meaning for me, my attention was drawn to them in a way it had not been before, and I felt more engaged in the activity of exploring them. Anytime we learn something new, the new territory of knowledge *out there* is annexed to the already existing body of knowledge we hold *inside* of us because some aspect of the knowledge or the way it's represented is able to act as a bridge. I was able to find the bridge that gave me some hope of at least visiting what lay on the other side of it—only after taking a good look at my process of coding.

While my method of learning Chinese words may seem idiosyncratic, some recent linguistic research indicates that our neural patterns for storing language are highly idiosyncratic. World-famous scientist Francis Crick, codiscoverer of the double-helix structure of DNA, also did research indicating that each person's coding of language is as individual as his or her fingerprints. Each individual has a unique neural pattern underlying his or her language ability. Through their studies of brain activity during language use, Dr. Crick and his team at the Salk Institute in La Jolla, California, found that different aspects of language are processed in different areas of the brain. In contrast to what was previously believed, there is not just one language center in the left brain that is activated when words are heard, spoken, or thought of; rather, a variety of different centers spread throughout the brain's visual and auditory cortices are activated simultaneously, and the relevant information from each converges to form the full meaning of the word with all relevant implications. One linguistic center might provide information about the spelling of the word, another about its part of speech, another about the appearance of the thing it represents. As MIT researcher Steven Pinker writes in his renowned book *The Language Instinct*:

Why has it been so hard to draw an atlas of the brain with areas for different parts of language? According to one school of thought, it is because there aren't any. . . . [E]xcept for sensation and movement, mental processes are patterns of neuronal activity that are widely distributed, hologram-style, all over the brain.

Whatever principle organizes all this diverse information and causes it to converge in a meaningful way, even to form a simple concept like "cup," for example, is still a mystery; however, Dr. Crick postulates that this as yet undiscovered, *binding* principle mediates meaningful language and perhaps all forms of cognition.

Similarly, neurosurgeon Dr. George Ojemann of the University of Washington found different people had language centers scattered in different parts of their brains. While Ojemann found that certain general tendencies existed in people with higher or lower verbal IQs (naming sites in those with high verbal IQs are located in the middle temporal gyrus, while those with less verbal ability have them in their parietal lobes), he found that language centers in the brain are idiosyncratically scattered in different places in different people. Steven Pinker writes of one of Dr. Ojemann's experiments in *The Language Instinct:*

Ojemann . . . found that stimulating within a site no more than a few millimeters across could disrupt a single [linguistic] function, like repeating or completing a sentence, naming an object, or reading a word. But these dots were scattered over the brain . . . and were found in different places in different people.

Dr. Ojemann's observation that people with high verbal IQs tend to store linguistic information in the middle temporal gyrus is also interesting in that the superior temporal gyrus was shown to be unusually active in those who experience colored-language synesthesia, according to studies of the British research team led by Dr. Simon Baron-Cohen. Perhaps colored-language synesthetes tend toward a particular general language processing pattern, albeit with the individual variations common to all neural patterns.

The brain, it seems, is a much more dynamic and plastic environment than was once believed, a place of great movement and interaction. In some people, language centers have been located not only in the left brain, but also in the right brain. Sometimes a second language can shift from the left brain to the right brain with the person's developing use of it, as has been shown in bilingual people before and after training as simultaneous interpreters.

Our understanding of even one single word of a language is a dynamic and complex process that arouses a whole host of neurons whose simultaneous firing forms a pattern unlike that in any other human brain. "A word," says Dr. Ojemann, "is a bundle of different kinds of information." A *New York Times* article titled "Brain Yields New Clues on Its Organization for Language" reported: "[W]hen a person thinks of a cup [for example], clusters of neurons that store knowledge of its attributes, like color, shape and texture, are activated and project their information onto a common convergence zone." Given this model, it is not hard to imagine that in synesthetes, some of the brain's visual areas, notably those used for storing information about visual details of objects—like area V4 in the ventral aspect of the temporal lobe—are also activated, adding color, texture, or other sensory information to the "mix," which forms the final "picture."

While synesthetes' way of storing linguistic information may involve neurons from unexpected visual centers of the brain, it is important to keep in mind that *every* individual's pattern of linguistic storage—whether that individual is synesthetic or nonsynesthetic—is unique, one-of-a-kind, unrepeated in any other human brain on earth. Researchers Crick and Ojemann discovered the unique aspect of neural patterning underlying linguistic processing through reports of neurosurgeons and through studies involving functional magnetic resonance imaging (MRI), which can show areas of neural activity during particular behavioral tasks.

Our neural patterns not only indicate how we process information but may also have implications for our chances for recovery from brain injuries such as those produced by stroke. In his foreword to this book, Dr. Peter Grossenbacher mentions some researchers' speculations that colored-language synesthetes might recover faster than many nonsynesthetes would from strokes affecting their verbal ability; for synesthetes, language is also stored in areas of the brain controlling visual information—areas that remain unaffected by the stroke. Thus, those linguistic/visual storage areas could allow the synesthete stroke victim to maintain a sense of language and to use what is maintained to retrieve and rebuild those linguistic functions lost to the stroke. Such aided recovery of stroke affecting verbal ability has been found among literate speakers of Chinese. Because the Chinese language is so pictorial in nature, literate speakers of the Chinese language store language in their right as well as their left brain. The areas in the right brain unaffected by a stroke causing damage to language centers in the left brain can be a great aid to the stroke victim in retrieving lost verbal ability.

While, as Dr. Ojemann tells us, certain areas of the brain may be particularly predisposed toward language function, many others can take over if needed. Other parts of the brain can learn to compensate and take over some functions formerly performed by the damaged areas. The brain's plasticity has been made particularly vivid in a recent animal study in which a ferret's neurons were rewired so that visual inputs to the retina landed in the auditory cortex instead of the visual cortex. The visual inputs eventually altered the auditory cortex so that it physically resembled and behaved like the visual cortex! So although particular parts of the brain may be predisposed toward certain specific functions, in adapting to environmental changes, they are capable of taking on very different functions.

Steven Pinker makes the point that such compensations routinely occur in the developing human brain. If, for example, any of the areas predisposed for wiring language suffer even minor damage, those circuits can grow in other parts of the brain. As he writes in *The Language Instinct*:

Many neurologists believe that this is why the language centers are located in unexpected places in a significant minority of people. Birth is traumatic. . . . The birth canal squeezes the baby's head like a lemon, and newborns frequently suffer small strokes and other brain insults. Adults with anomalous language areas may be the recovered victims of these primal injuries . . . which . . . bespeak no ill effects.

Such minor injuries can affect individual brain development and contribute to the individual's unique neural pattern for coding language.

But regardless of the possible causes of our unique mechanisms for coding language—or indeed, any kind of information—the mechanisms themselves may be consciously employed as learning tools. The first step, of course, is to become aware of what those mechanisms, or ways of coding, are.

People with synesthesia become particularly aware of their internal mechanisms for coding information when they discover that most other people find this way of coding unusual. Before making this discovery, most synesthetes will tell you that they never much thought about how they were processing information—they simply took their processes for granted, as most people do, assuming their experience was more or less like everyone else's. It is only when synesthetes receive surprised reactions to their perceptions that they begin to examine those perceptions more closely—and it seems that there are benefits to be gained from this close examination, which all of us could reap if we became better acquainted with our methods of personal coding. Look more closely and you may be surprised to find how very attached you are to those perceptions and coding mechanisms that constitute your inner landscape.

Psychologist Raymond Wheeler, who studied synesthesia back in the 1920s with his subject, Thomas Cutsforth, concluded in a paper entitled "The Synesthesia of a Blind Subject" that "synesthesia functions in the same way as certain unattended mental processes in nonsynesthetes. It happens that colors instead of other kinds of processes may be aspects of the larger whole." What would happen if those "unattended" mental processes were attended to?

What could our personal codes reveal if we took time to look at and better know the dynamic coding processes that are there at every moment? Perhaps parts of our hidden code reveal themselves externally in places where we do our creative work: studios, offices, workshops.

I think of my father's basement workshop with the nuggets of the world's wisdom penned on its walls in subdued graffiti style:

> Our life is frittered away by detail. . . . Simplify, simplify.
> —Thoreau

> He is great who is what he is from nature
> and never reminds us of others.
> —Emerson

> Consciousness is a complete miracle.
> —George Bernard Shaw

> Know thyself.
> —Oracle at Delphi

The basement workshop was an externalization of the deeply fecund inner space that was my father's creative mind. It was the place where he created a range of things, from perpetual motion machines to birdhouses to dollhouses that illustrated the wonders of electromagnetism to a primitive version of a telephone answering machine. ("That's crazy, Dad!" we all said back in 1961. "Nobody would ever let a machine answer the phone!") In his workshop, my father felt free to do his experiments against the backdrop of his own landscape of personal meaning. What appears vividly in my own mind now is a certain space on the workshop wall with the scrawled quote from the ancient Oracle at Delphi: "Know thyself."

chapter nine

THE VARIETIES OF INTELLIGENCE AND PERSONAL CODING STYLES

*The scraps of memory—that is all they are—that stay with us
after a dream seem illogical only to superficial observers, on whom
the splendid power and beauty of this kingdom are lost.*

—ALFRED KUBIN, *THE OTHER SIDE*

Alfred Kubin, an early twentieth-century German artist, spent a
miserable youth in his small Austrian village of Zell, where he
was regarded as entirely unpromising by his father and by everyone
else. In *Autobiography of Alfred Kubin,* Kubin relates his humiliating
expulsion from school:

*In my second year, I failed completely. Mathematics and Latin were my
particular bugbears—I tried to substitute novels about Indians and desert
islands for these hated subjects. My father had lost all confidence in me. I
returned home a miserable failure. . . . I experienced for the first time, a
period of real hell. Every day I got up early and took a long walk in the
mountains so that children and grown-ups might not witness the shameful
sight of a student expelled from Latin school.*

Kubin's young life was filled with loneliness and rejection; however, the long, solitary walks he took to escape his feelings of disgrace
also served to put him more in touch with his inner world of images,

which helped him blossom into the celebrated artist he eventually became. As Kubin grew from adolescence to young manhood, his father finally, and fortunately, recognized his son's artistic inclinations and sent him to the Art Academy in Munich. Once he was out of his provincial village and in the city, Kubin had access to the great collections of art in Munich's top museums and galleries. He discovered the fantastic works of Max Klinger, Odilon Redon, and Pieter Breughel. Breughel's *Garden of Earthly Delights* depicted dimensions of consciousness that matched Kubin's own longing to code his inner world of dreams. Having the chance to view such great works of art opened up a whole new dimension of possibility for Kubin. He now felt empowered to develop and create his own art of the inner life.

Kubin created an illustrated novel called *The Other Side*, about an artist who spent a good deal of his time in the Dream Kingdom. His novel, illustrated with pen and ink drawings, received much critical and popular acclaim in the artistic world of turn-of-the-century Berlin. A top Berlin gallery gave the young artist a one-man exhibition of his work when Kubin was just twenty-five years old.

Kubin possessed an ability that Harvard University's educational innovator Howard Gardner might classify as "intrapersonal intelligence," a type that went largely unrecognized and uncultivated for much of the artist's life. Gardner defines intrapersonal intelligence as having "knowledge of the internal aspects of a person, access to one's own feeling life, and the capacity to discriminate the range of emotions and to represent this knowledge through some written or artistic means." It is one of the seven types of intelligence that Gardner has identified in his influential book *Multiple Intelligences*. He argues that many kinds of abilities go unnoticed in children because of modern society's bias in favor of mathematical-logical ability and its tendency to judge overall intelligence by it. He suggests methods for testing and identifying all the major forms of intelligence, lest they go unrecognized and thus undeveloped in children. In addition to intrapersonal, Gardner identifies six other types of intelligence as:

1. **Bodily-kinesthetic intelligence:** the ability to develop specialized body movements, which have obvious advantages for human adaptation.

2. **Logical-mathematical intelligence:** the ability to do problem solving encased in abstract, sequential forms, such as mathematical equations.

3. **Linguistic intelligence:** the ability to put thought processes into meaningful syntax so as to transmit them as accurately as possible to others. As Gardner writes, "The gift of language is universal, and its development is strikingly constant across cultures. Even in deaf populations where a manual sign language is not taught, children will often 'invent' their own manual language and use it surreptitiously! *We thus see how an intelligence can operate independently of a specific input modality or output channel*" (italics mine; the latter statement also could be applied to the understanding of colored-language synesthesia).

4. **Spatial intelligence:** the ability to navigate and use notational systems of maps and the ability to visualize three-dimensional objects from different angles.

5. **Musical intelligence:** the ability to perceive and create patterns of sound, a capacity that plays an important role in unifying societies and even species (as birdsong does), and to represent the pattern of sound with a symbolic notational system.

6. **Interpersonal intelligence:** the ability to notice core distinctions in the temperaments, moods, and motivations of others and to read unspoken intentions and form strategies of interaction.

Gardner feels it is vital for society to identify and cultivate the various types of intelligence of its members so as to increase the chances of finding solutions to social problems. He writes:

[O]ur world is beset by problems; to have any chance of solving them, we must make the very best of the intelligences we possess. Perhaps recognizing the plurality of intelligences and the manifold ways in which human individuals may exhibit them is an important first step.

Gardner argues that our society has long had a certain academic bias in favor of recognizing and measuring mathematical-logical intelligence and against acknowledging and cultivating other forms. I feel that in concert with this bias, perhaps, is the bias toward presenting and coding information in a particular way. As we saw in Chapter One, an individual's personal coding falls away as it is replaced by the socially endorsed standard code of society.

Certainly, this is true of many children who lose much of their ability to visualize as they get older. Studies show the ability to conjure up mental imagings starts to wax and then wane as children develop within an educational system that emphasizes a more abstract and less pictorial mode of thinking.

Similarly, the one-third of children whom studies show experience synesthetic imagery often lose much if not all of it in adapting to the prevailing abstract, unisensory code. So, whether a given child's personal way of coding is synesthetic or nonsynesthetic, it can become far less vivid if it conflicts with the standard norm of information coding.

Obviously, it is important for children to learn a shared code for representing information. Society could not exist without such a code. But just as we would never want to lose our first language when we learn a second one (as there are obvious benefits to knowing both), so might we discover benefits to keeping our personal code alive even after we have learned the shared one. Just as each of the world's languages is far more than an arbitrary sound system, but rather, is a unique cultural worldview, so a personal code is a unique individual worldview. An individual's personal way of coding information is a unique, one-of-a-kind way of thinking about and perceiving the world.

At this point, we may wonder whether David Hockney could have painted and assembled the vivid stage sets for the Metropolitan Opera if he had "outgrown" the capacity for seeing music coded in color. Because some innovators retained awareness of their personal code, they were able to express things that might otherwise have remained forever unexpressed. Retaining awareness of one's personal code could present definite benefits not only to the individual but also to the community.

People with synesthesia become particularly aware of their way of coding only when they realize most people are not coding in the same way. This realization usually comes by accident: synesthetic artist Carol Steen casually mentioned seeing a pretty pink A; composer Michael Torke told his mother he wanted to practice his "blue piece" of music today; the four-year-old Nabokov complained to his mother that the colors on his alphabet blocks were "all wrong." It is only the surprised reaction of others that makes synesthetes begin to reflect on their own way of coding. They attend to it when they realize it is different. As we have seen, this greater attention to the personal code often has quite productive and creative results: We may recall Carol Steen mining her synesthetic sensations for images to use in her paintings and sculpture; Richard Feynman employing them to "see" mathematical concepts (which he wondered how his students were "seeing"); Ruth Armer painting the visual form music took in her mind; Marcia Smilack listening to the colorful musical crescendo in her head to know when to snap the shutter and create her camera paintings; and Natasha Lvovich using her colored words as tools in learning multiple foreign languages.

While synesthetes have a "dual-sensory" mode of coding, and nonsynesthetes code information in discrete sensory modes, each person's code is unique. I tutor some (nonsynesthetic) students of English as a second language and have asked them to observe some of their own ways of coding. Are those ways visual, auditory, or kinesthetic, and how exactly does the code manifest? One reported how learning to put correct stress on words in an English sentence caused her to feel a pressure in one or another shoulder. Recalling the feeling of pressure helped her to retrieve elusive, correctly stressed phrases from her memory. Another student told of remembering new words and phrases she had learned by feeling the rhythm of the phrases in her body—then retrieving the actual words. Remembering the rhythm would help bring the verbal aspect to her conscious mind.

Similarly, (nonsynesthete) painter Sebastian King reports feeling "a certain muscular tension" when trying to retrieve an elusive name from his memory. The tension takes the form of a mental image of a car struggling uphill. When the road "evens out," the "hidden" name flashes into consciousness. Another painter, Maria de Echevarria, recalls a moment when she felt very moved; the feeling took the form of, as she says, "a continuum of intangible bubbles inside and around me." This visceral image blossomed into a fully realized "memory painting" called "Madeleines." Poet and painter Laura Glenn reports seeing an image of mist in her mind when searching for an elusive word. She has a sense of walking through the mist, looking for it. When she finds the word, the mist lifts. (See page 94.)

These examples parallel synesthetes' common experience of remembering the color of the word or name in question before the word or name itself. All of us code information in one or more sensory modes. We may recall that as far back as 1920, psychologist Raymond Wheeler, working with his blind subject and fellow researcher Thomas Cutsforth, concluded that there was no such thing as image-less, sensation-less meaning and that all people code information in particular sensory modes. As historian Kevin Dann reports in *Bright Colors Falsely Seen*, "Wheeler and Cutsforth showed that synesthesia is not a phenomenon of perception alone, but of conception; synesthesia is an essential mechanism in the construction of meaning that functions in the same way as certain unattended mental processes in nonsynesthetes."

Wheeler and Cutsforth concluded that the way we process information becomes part and parcel of it: Form is part of content. Since everything has form and content, neither element is arbitrary. Just as Dann writes, "Synesthetes experience their own synesthesia as a form of thinking," so all people experience their particular mental imagery, or kinesthetic sensations, as a form of thinking.

Yet many of us are only vaguely conscious of how we process and conceive of information. When I first ask students or friends the question, "What does knowledge look like or sound like or feel like to you?," I am usually met with blank stares. We often feel that knowledge and understanding have an invisible presence in our minds. When asked what a piece of information looks like, people will often answer, "It doesn't look like anything." Perhaps that's true, for not everyone is a "visual coder." However, it is likely that even the information that we do code visually hovers unnoticed around the edges of our consciousness—though it might be triggered by the right stimulus. In his magnificent literary work *Remembrance of Things Past*, Marcel Proust depicts the wealth of scenes that appear in the mind of the narrator, triggered by the taste of the French biscuit, the madeleine, soaked in lime tea. Kevin Dann would call Marcel's memory an instance of eidetic memory, which Dann describes in the following way:

[I]n eideticism, a normal, subjective visual image is experienced with particular vividness; although not dependent on the experience of an actual external object, the eidetic image is seen inside the mind and is accompanied by bodily engagement with the image; the experience of the eidetic image is a healthy, not pathological structure; like the photisms of colored hearing and other synesthetic percepts, the eidetic image is noteworthy for its vividness and memorability.

The taste of a madeleine soaked in lime tea triggered an eidetic childhood memory for Marcel. The taste, which Marcel had not

known since taking tea at his aunt's house in the village of his childhood, had the power to revive the dormant world of his past:

*And suddenly the memory revealed itself. The taste was that of the little piece
of madeleine which on Sunday mornings at Combray . . . when I went to say
good morning to her in her bedroom, my Aunt Leonie used to give me,
dipping it first in her own cup of tea. . . . And as soon as I had recognised
the taste of the piece of madeleine soaked in her decoction of lime-blossom
which my aunt used to give me . . . immediately the old grey house upon the
street, where her room was, rose up like a stage set . . . and the good folk of
the village and their little dwellings and the parish church and the whole of
Combray and its surroundings, taking shape and solidity, sprang into being,
town and gardens alike, from my cup of tea.*

Just as Marcel could not taste the lime tea–soaked madeleine
without its triggering the memory of his town, so can I not read
Proust's passage without its triggering the memory of my brother. My
brother, Jackie, loved this passage from Proust's novel because I
believe he saw in the narrator's experience a reflection of his own.
Jackie, too, seemed to have an eidetic memory. He was able to recall
very vivid details from our childhood, prompted by hearing music we
used to listen to as children or even by just remembering foods we
used to eat. When he died prematurely of cancer at age forty-four, I
felt that my childhood had shrunk; I had depended on Jackie to be
the keeper of our common memories, so together we could re-create
and relive the comedies and dramas of the theater of our childhood.

Dann writes that eidetic memory and synesthesia often go
together. The two can sometimes be found within the same families
and in the same individuals, as they were in Nabokov. Some say
Nabokov's powerful eidetic memory enabled him to write the precise,
vivid prose that was the hallmark of his novels.

Although many minds may be capable of retrieving vivid visual
scenes, I believe it's also true that visualizing may not be everyone's

internal method of coding. Some may code information aurally; it may sound like something in the mind's ear more often than it may look like something in the mind's eye. Some may, for example, remember key lines from a professor's lecture, so that the information is coded in the sound of a person's voice.

In the 1980s and 1990s, educational researchers such as Rebecca Oxford of the University of Maryland and Anita Wenden of York College in New York stressed the importance of identifying different learning styles: Visual learners needed to see information, perhaps written out or displayed in the form of pictures or diagrams in order to best absorb and retain it; auditory learners needed to hear information spoken, explained, or perhaps even set to music; tactile learners needed a more hands-on approach. The better acquainted individual learners are with how they are taking in and processing information, the better they can take charge of their own learning and use their self-knowledge to learn more efficiently and independently. Perhaps we could take the insights of researchers into learning styles one step further and consider precisely how information manifests in the mind of a visual, or an auditory or a tactile, learner. Visual learners might be encouraged to write or draw the way they code information for deposit into their memory banks, an auditory learner might reflect upon just how and in what form words or sounds reverberate in the mind's ear when information is stored or retrieved, and tactile learners might notice which muscles they must move in order to absorb or access information.

In the 1980s, proponents of neurolinguistic programming suggested our everyday word choice in conversation could offer a clue as to our dominant mode of absorbing, storing, and retrieving information. Visual learners tend to say that they "see" when they agree, while tactile learners might tell you that they *feel* the same way and auditory learners might assert, "Yeah, I hear you!"

By getting more in touch with those vague, ephemeral images, sensations or inner hearings that creep quietly in our awareness on little cat's feet, perhaps we can use them as triggers to more quickly retrieve information from our memories, or as starting blocks on which we can build new concepts and creations. Certainly, the artist Alfred Kubin sensed the power of such fragments of thought and dream as ways back to stored knowledge or forward to new creativity.

Researcher Dr. Roger Watt of the University of Stirling makes the point that our diverse ways of thinking and perceiving could have a salutary effect from an evolutionary point of view. In an interview on the BBC program *Orange Sherbet Kisses*, he said:

Maybe [difference in perception] is part of an evolutionary beneficial process. . . . [I]t could be the case that we develop different neural structures [so that] our personalized perceptions develop. Consequently, you have the possibility that different people will see a better way of going about things. In other words, people with perceptions that are different are more likely to be able to become creative in particular circumstances.

On the Internet synesthesia list, there is sometimes discussion as to whether the trait of synesthesia, as a manifestation of the evolutionary process, is increasing in the human population and, if so, whether this is a positive thing. In response to this concern, Sean Day, who runs the list, says the important thing is not whether the evolutionary process creates more or fewer synesthetes, but that it creates *both* synesthetes *and* nonsynesthetes. As he commented on the list on February 24, 2000:

[A]s far as synesthesia and humans go, we can say that, in general, an increase in diversity helps to insure [sic] that at least some members of the species will survive change to environs, disasters and so on. . . . [W]hat is most beneficial to humans as a species is not synesthesia, nor is it a lack of synesthesia; rather, what is best is that we have both people with and without synesthesia!

It may be beneficial both to ourselves and to those around us if each of us, synesthete or nonsynesthete, takes the time to explore the many diverse ways we code information to remember and to develop our knowledge. The following are some simple questions that may give some clue as to how you code information.

Think of an important event in your life (perhaps a celebration such as a birthday or marriage, but any significant event will do). What do you see, hear, or otherwise experience in your mind's eye or ear? Do scenes, sounds, tastes, or other physical sensations come into your mind? Do you find yourself smiling at certain memories? Apart from the muscles around your lips and mouth, are you aware of any other muscular movements in your body as you remember the day? Think about an idea you found interesting. How does the idea appear to you? Are there images or words connected to this idea in your mind's eye? If so, do you see the words written out, or do you hear them being spoken? If you see them written, what do they look like? Are the words printed or handwritten? Are they on a page or floating free in the space of your mind's eye? If you hear the words, who is speaking them? Is it the voice of someone you know? Is it your voice? Think about your name. What comes into your mind? Does your name look like something in your mind's eye? What does it look like? Do you hear someone saying your name? Whose voice do you hear? Is there a visual scene that accompanies it?

Kubin saw the power in dream fragments to lead us back to important knowledge. The catalog to a 1968 showing of Kubin's work at The Galerie St. Etienne in New York (quoted from Kubin's *The Other Side*) states, "If the fragments of dream that remain in the . . . mind could somehow be reassembled . . . reconstituted in the conscious world, we might capture not only the secret of art, but of life, itself." (See page 95.)

Whether or not retrieving fragments of memory helps us find the secret of art and of life, it may at the very least help us retrieve useful knowledge and building blocks for new creations. If we retain the language of personal coding, we can use it for absorbing, retrieving, and retaining new information or perhaps reassembling it in a creative way. By retaining our personal coding, perhaps more of us will fulfill the statement of Alfred Kubin, artist and reassembler of dreams, who hoped that each person would be able to "create what he must, in his own fashion, to the extent that his gift permits."

chapter ten

A YEAR IS A STRING
OF TWELVE COLORED RECTANGLES

Time is space.

For many synesthetes, time *is* space. Units of time are experienced internally as places, three-dimensional landscapes with color, texture, shape, perspective. A year is a yellow triangle with sharp corners turning from December to January. A week is a ladder with rungs of color for each day of the week. Or it is a coiled spiral with colors emanating outward, spinning off into larger color spirals to form a constellation of months forming a multi-hued year.

I have always thought of time as a place and did not even think to connect this to my synesthesia until Dr. Peter Grossenbacher told me he'd found that a number of colored-language synesthetes also reported perceiving time as having color, shape, and dimension. Although Simon Baron-Cohen feels that the experience of colored time does not fit into a conventional definition of synesthesia (that is, when one sense is stimulated, more than one responds), Dr. Grossenbacher views the perception of colored time as "conceptual synesthesia": Synesthetes have an automatic, consistent, full sensory notion of time units, which for most people are abstract. In addition, the colors that a given synesthete perceives for a month or day of the week or year often match the colors she or he perceives for the name of that month, day, or year.

For me, weeks, months, and the year are landscapes that pop up absolutely unbidden if I think about the "whens" of my life: when I have to go to work, meet a friend, sit down to write, get away for a weekend. I can't conceive of time apart from its landscapes: A week is a colored pathway, a kind of sidewalk with seven squares of colored pavement. I need to qualify that description, however, because the material that composes my week's sidewalk doesn't have the hardness of concrete; its substance seems outside the realm of hardness or softness as it is, quite literally, "solid color." The part of my mind where the week-path exists takes the notion of solid color seriously. I glide along the week-path from one solid colored square to the next to get from day to day. At either end of my week are the double white squares of Saturday and Sunday (although each is a different shade of white). The Saturday and Sunday squares are white because the words "Saturday" and "Sunday" are white. Saturday, however, is a very bright white because it is "lit up" by the sunny influence of the two orange A's and lighter orange R in the word "Saturday." These two shades of orange potentiate each other, lighting up the whole of Saturday's "territory" with an orange sunlight that emanates from the word's orange letters. The Sunday square, on the other hand, is a more staid white. The sparkle of its initial letter S is subdued by the serious brown of its U and its extreme dark brown N and somber brown D. These brown letters also potentiate each other to create a more somber and static ambiance in the Sunday space.

　　Although I glide from Saturday to Sunday, I jump, or step down, from Sunday to Monday, whose brown square is on a lower part of the sidewalk-path. Brown Monday is even a darker brown than its initial letter M, which is a dark tan. The word's darker color is influenced by its very dark brown N and the darker D. In addition, I wonder if the fact that Monday can sometimes feel like a dark and difficult day for me has also lent a certain emotional reinforcement to its darker shade of brown. From Monday, I glide to navy blue Tuesday, whose dark shade of blue is influenced by its brown U and D; then it's on to yellow-brown Wednesday, which spreads itself wider than the other days, emphasizing its special status as the middle of the week. From light brown Wednesday, it's a downward glide to blue-jay blue Thursday, whose lighter blue is influenced by its orange-yellow H and light orange R. Another glide and it's on to smoky, silver-gray Friday, from whose narrow patch of gray territory I fall into bright, white Saturday, all lit up with orange sunlight.

As I describe the days of the week, I realize one could make a case for emotional influences that reinforce their colors: Certainly when I was a child, Saturday was a bright, happy day that I was likely to spend outdoors in the sunlight, which may account for the greater influence of certain of Saturday's brighter letters like its two orange A's and R, rather than its darker-colored U and D; Sunday was a more somber day; the day for going to church and doing homework and getting ready to wake up early on dark brown Monday.

I glide along my week to get to the day I'm talking about or thinking about, just the way I glide along my alphabet trail to get to the letter I need. If on Monday I say to someone, "Let's meet for lunch on Thursday," I see us in the distance, standing together in the middle of the blue-jay blue square that is Thursday. If we are planning to meet for dinner, I see us on the upper part of the square, but if our appointment is for lunch, we are on the lower-middle part of the square. If we are meeting at 7 P.M., a green 7 comes into focus with the two of us alongside it, as the scene dissolves into that of the place we are to meet. So perhaps my week is a kind of abstract map fusing together personal and objective content. I might see the friend I'm going to meet on, say, the blue Thursday square and glide over to it as if we were already there together. If I have to take a subway to meet the friend on Thursday, the blue square where I see us standing will open up into the Manhattan cityscape with the subway entrance's green neon bulbs atop its blackish-green poles signaling the downward flight of cement steps.

A synesthete and researcher into the anthropology of synesthesia, Ian Watson, points out that color coding is a very common social convention for identifying and categorizing a whole range of social

activities from baseball teams to national flags. Watson views synesthetes' color coding of time units simply as an extension of this social
convention. In a paper titled "The Common Triggers of Synesthesia
are Social Conventions," Watson writes:

> [T]he alphanumeric, calendrical, and musical systems that commonly trigger
> synesthesia are each made up of a set of conventional units. Learning to
> distinguish and interpret these units is not a universal psychodevelopmental
> process, but rather, a product of our cognitive socialization. Assigning color
> tags to these units reinforces their sometimes dubious distinctiveness. And
> common synesthesia is only one of many ways in which we use experientially
> primary contrasts like color to tag socially conventional categories.

As mentioned previously, in analyzing my own colored time
units, I can sometimes notice the influence of socialization in the correspondence between a given day's colors and its emotional tone
(Monday, dark brown; Saturday, sunlit orange-white).

What is startling to me, however, is the fact that my mind came
up with this color-coded land of time so *automatically*, so sponta-
neously without my doing anything at all to invent it. In this way,
synesthesia operates a bit like a dream to manufacture places and
scenes—although while places in dreams generally manifest only
once in our experience, my land of time has been with me in its present form since childhood and I cannot imagine ever being without it.

Although landscapes of weeks, months, years, and even days and
hours have woven themselves in my mind the way dreams do, they are
never temporary and fleeting like dreams, but are with me always, a
part of my mind's permanent collection. I feel, however, that whatever
mechanism of mind creates the dreamscapes of sleep could also create these timescapes of waking life.

Kevin Dann calls synesthesia a form of thinking, which my own
experience corroborates; certainly, I cannot think about time apart
from my colored pathways, and I have trouble understanding how it's

possible for anyone not to conceive of units of time without seeing them as places. I remember how surprised I was when I asked my father what Monday looked like to him and he said that, for him, Monday didn't look like anything; I cannot imagine time being a thing I couldn't see, a place I couldn't go to. For some synesthetes, internal timescapes can be very useful, as in the case of a young woman from Columbia University who told me she had no need ever to look at a calendar because her visualization of time was so clear in her mind's eye.

Judy de Chantal, writing on the Internet synesthesia list, also describes time as a place. This is a description of her year:

My current year runs vertical. . . . If I am thinking about February, I am standing right at the bottom looking up at the next days in the month. Meanwhile, March, April, May, June, etc. are stacked at the top. They are tightly stacked till July-August-September when they stretch fat and very light. If I [need] to look at September, I step to the left, bottom corner of September and have a good look [at the whole month].

If someone walks up to me and says I'll see you next Wednesday, I have to flip the week over. . . . Guess what I am saying is, until I actually go there and see it in my head, it doesn't register very well.

Similarly, Kerryo Oen, another writer on the synesthesia list, describes his time-place:

I have a complex temporal framework. My year is a triangle roughly divided into unequal sized months. The corners are at December/January and "June-ish," not quite July. There is a "zoom" at the December turn. The week concept is an oval with days of unequal lengths. It turns the corner in the middle of Saturday and again in the middle of Sunday. . . . The day is an oval as well which turns the corner at midnight and somewhere around six in the morning. It spirals (an oval spiral) into the week. I have a holding spot beside June, where I stay usually, and when I think of a date, I move there.

Another synesthete describes her years to fellow synesthetes on the list as the following:

My years are sort of like ladders spread out on the ground in various directions, depending on which year we are in. . . . [T]he rungs of the ladders are the months and are different colors, textures, etc. The ladders themselves are different colors, depending on which year it is. I "run" and stand in various positions around these ladders to have a "look" at the months, etc., depending on what I am thinking about. For instance, if I am thinking about 1981, I "run and stand" with my toes touching January and I look up to December. January is a big dark red and navy blue space between the rungs.

Christina McAllister's description of her year shows just how unusual and how precise a synesthete's time vision can be:

. . . My year is roughly shaped like a sneaker (with the toe pointing to the right) or loaf of bread with one end much higher. Starting in the lower right corner, draw a sweeping, slightly curved line to the west, then vertical about one third of the other length, then to the NNE a line about a third of the last and then head SE about two thirds of the original line, slightly curved and then angle SSE to meet the start of the original line. It would be much easier to draw than to explain in words!

Another writer to the synesthesia list, identified only as Elizabeth, writes:

I tried to explain my year to my family once because I wanted to know how they saw years, but none of them knew what I was talking about. My year is also an oval, like an 'O' on its side, but thinner. Just seeing the shape of a year in general makes it yellow, maybe because O's are yellow. Anyway, New Year's is at 12 o'clock, the summer months (June, July, August) stretch from about 8 o'clock to 5 o'clock. My year does run counterclockwise, who knows why. From 8 to 5 it is a bright pink color, while around 12 (Jan.) is a nice green color.

My week is a little simpler. The weekends are tall dark rectangles while weekdays are squares. They are all together in a horizontal row. I am kind of apprehensive about the next millennium (even though I know it doesn't officially start yet), just because of the change in numbers. While 9 (and therefore the 1900s) are a safe, soft, black, 2 is a silvery, white, shiny number. It's really something I don't want to think about—having white, silvery stuff everywhere.

These descriptions have the complexity and idiosyncrasy of dreams. That same mysterious, unconscious part of ourselves that spins out dreamscapes by night may also be spinning out visions of aesthetically pleasing, functional timescapes by day, weaving together the synesthete's time-colors, life routines with their own mood responses to them.

When it comes to thinking about what I have to do *today*, I am so in the day that I can't see its shape. Even the day's color subsides to make way for the "colored number" hours (a green 2:00, a dark red 3:00, and so on) that hang suspended in higher places ahead of me or behind me in lower portions of the day. It's the colors of the hours that I see when I'm in the day; the day has color only when I get some perspective on it, standing back to see it as part of the week's big picture. As I write this, I am in Newport, Rhode Island, and I am also next to a big green, red, and white 2:30 P.M., which is suspended in the grayish air of today. Up above in the distance I see a smaller soft purple 5 P.M., the time I have to catch my bus to go back to New York. Up above the purple 5, I see a big orange, gray, soft purple 9:45 P.M., the time the bus will pull into the Port Authority New York Bus Terminal, and higher still, white 10 P.M., which is the time I expect to turn the key to my apartment door and arrive home.

At the very top of today, I see white/green 12 midnight, the time I expect to go to sleep; then the day peaks and I have to go down a slope and watch the hour numbers go down to the bottom of the next morning when the alarm will ring at yellow and red 6:30 A.M. The yellow of the 6 is more vivid than the red of the 3, not only because 6 comes first, but because the yellow of 6 matches the yellow of the morning sun.

In the months of my year, too, I can see how this combination of synesthetic letters and numbers, as well as some social conventions relevant to my own life, have influenced the formation of its landscape. My year is an oblong shape with twelve colored rectangles, one for each month. (See page 97.) As I write this chapter, it's the start of November, so I am just past the border of the green and white rectangle of October, a few steps into November's patch of deep brown, warmed up by its cranberry-colored V and vibrant red E's and lighter brown M. Did the color of Thanksgiving cranberries heighten the importance of the word's cranberry-colored V? Then I move into December, a lighter and warmer patch of brown on the year's path with its two red E's, light brown M, and deep blue C. As I approach the farther part of December's territory later in the month, I see the sparkle of Christmas ornaments: December's patch of territory can open into real holiday scenes of Christmas tree lots and shoppers hurrying along snowy New York City streets. As I walk the very last steps of December's territory, I turn a corner and cross over the border to the black pool of January with its red garnet frame. It was puzzling to me why January, a blue-colored word, would translate into a black and garnet red month on my calendar-path: It was almost like the mystery of why some verbs take on irregular forms. I remember the little garnet-stone ring on the finger of Patsy Ronayne, my first childhood best friend, whose birthday was on January 31. Could this memory have colored the cold, sunless month of January, turning it from a blue-jay blue word into a black, garnet red–bordered month?

Crossing the border of black and garnet January, I reach foggy February, gray and smoky like its initial letter F. Its rectangle is narrower than those of January or March, which surround it, perhaps because it is a shorter month. March is a large, brown month, but a darker brown than its initial M would indicate. I associate March with rain, perhaps because it is the month when New York City winter turns to spring and snow gives way to rain, coloring city sidewalks a shade of wet brown. April is an orange, yellow, and pink month, the orange and yellow coming from its orange A and pale yellow P, but there is some pink there, too, although none of its letters justify this. Perhaps it was the pink ribbons I used to find on my Easter baskets left by the bunny on Easter morning.

May is a calm light brown with a feeling of ease and stability. By May, springtime has really come and there is less tug-of-war with the cooler temperatures of leftover winter. It is also the month of my birthday, which in my childhood made for a calmer, more contented feeling than it does now!

June is a darker blue than the blue of its initial letter J, influenced by its brown U and N. July with its pale yellow L seems to open into the sunny ocean of Rockaway and Jones beaches, places my family drove to often in the summer days of my childhood. August is dark, glowing orange, a color even more intense than its initial letter justifies, probably influenced by the intense glowing sun of a sticky late summer in New York City. To get from August to September, I turn a corner and move from hot orange territory to a serious white space of room temperature. I walk into a flat white September, not sparkly like the letter S alone. It is more like the flat white of notebook or looseleaf paper, so associated with "back to school." Crossing the September border, I move into October, another white month with a border of green. I could not figure out why the green border was there (although October *does* contain a green B) until I realized that it might also be influenced by the green of 7, the date of my brother's October birthday and 28, the date of my father's (number 2 is also green).

It seems the mind creates its own mixture of shorthand, weaving elements of the societal and the subjective together to create its timescapes. This woven societal/subjective pattern is also fused with a spiritual element for synesthete Susan Hellerer, who identifies her profession as "ritual designer." Hellerer describes a sensation of literally feeling herself "in" time, moving *inside* an hour or a day, walking within a week, looking behind her at the "smaller," previous days or weeks as they recede in the distance. Hellerer feels that this experience of time helps in her work designing and choreographing creative ritual ceremonies, tailored to the personal desires and tastes of her clients as they move through one or another of life's passages: marriages, births, retirements. In addition, she designs ceremonies for women's life passages for which no formal rituals exist in our culture, such as menarche, menopause, and even divorce.

Many life passage rituals involve the concept of the "wheel of life"—which to Hellerer is not just an abstract concept, but an everyday reality. "The wheel of life, which is abstract for my students, is quite a literal experience for me," she says. "I always feel myself walking on the wheel of life because it's the way time looks and feels to me. It's not a metaphor at all, but a part of my daily experience." Hellerer, who holds a Master of Divinity degree from Union Theological Seminary, feels that the whole spiritual notion of "walking the labyrinth" came from the mind's capacity for experiencing time as a place. Hellerer also experiences the liturgical year as a place:

All the events on the liturgical year have choreography and color and I'll be describing it all to the students in my spiritual group called "Woman Wheel" and for a while, they'll be inspired. Though it's literal for me, my description of walking through the year sounds very imaginative to them. So the students will be interested, but then my description starts to go to a place where they can't follow anymore. I have to remember that I keep seeing and walking on my wheel year, but they don't.

Hellerer's description of teaching reminds me of physicist Richard Feynman's bafflement over "what the hell" the colored equations he was seeing as he lectured looked like to his students (who weren't "seeing" them). Hellerer connects her perception of colored patterns of words and time landscapes to a reverence she's always felt for life. "I began to realize at a certain point," she says, "that what my students were getting from my teaching had less to do with my knowledge of sacred ritual than with a sense they have of the way I perceive it. They feel my perception of things indicates I'm in touch with something they hope to find in themselves."

Although Hellerer says she very much values her way of seeing, she also reports having felt a certain guilt about it while growing up. "I knew I was not learning things the way my teachers wanted me to learn them," she says. "I was taking in information in a way that I wasn't supposed to, practicing a sort of 'trickery' my teachers wouldn't approve of." Some of her friends, too, seemed to disapprove of her "frivolous" way of perceiving:

I remember when I was eight years old, asking my best friend, "What do your letters and numbers do?" The friend looked at me as if I were crazy. I dropped the subject of "what numbers do" and never brought it up with her again. I began to see my three-dimensional letter, number, and time landscapes as a kind of "secret magic" that other people couldn't share and it made me feel like I was taking in information in a way that was wrong. In some ways, there's a certain pain in talking about these memories even now because they remind me of when I was little and people thought I was making them up or being very silly. I felt I had to hide the way I was internalizing things.

Just recently, I read an article in the *New York Times* that discussed how though people in different parts of China have different spoken dialects, they are linked by the pictorial ideograms of their common visual, written language. It occurs to me that synesthetes, too, are linked, but by the idiosyncratic imagery of their internal worlds;

although the colors, shapes, and dimensions of their respective landscapes may be different, just the fact that time and language are perceived as locales connects synesthetes with an instant recognition of common experience. To that wonderful, bonding phrase, "So you see what I see!" we may add a second, "So you go where I go!" Both phrases capture the flash of happy, relieved familiarity that says that although we synesthetes may be on different streets, we're all in the same city.

chapter eleven

SYNESTHESIA IN CYBERSPACE

The Internet was made for synesthetes.

—DR. PETER GROSSENBACHER

"Cyber-country" is the place where even the most nonstandard vision of things has a chance to make its presence known. Synesthetes have not been slow about giving voice to their visions on the Internet; since the 1990s, a host of sites have appeared, as well as the synesthesia list.

Sean Day's synesthesia list is an absolute "must" for anyone checking synesthesia cybercountry. This is the place where synesthetes get connected and chat, where unique "digital voices" combine to create an evolving synesthete culture. An associate professor of English with a Ph.D. from Purdue University, Sean Day founded and runs the list, which gives synesthetes from all over the world a forum in which to communicate about their perceptual experiences. Day started the site in 1992 after having enthusiastically participated in a linguistics list run by Purdue. He thought, "Why not a list for synesthetes?" Day is a synesthete who experiences colored music and plays a variety of instruments, including drums, guitar, xylophone, marimbas, vibraphone, organ, lute, and his favorite, the piano (he says the sound of a piano looks like "sky-blue cheap plastic"). He also enjoys listening to the colors of musical instruments he does not play, like the alto saxophone (its sounds look like "lit purple neon tubing"). Although he comes from a family in which nearly everyone plays music, he is the only member who hears it in color. Day has experienced colored music ever since he can remember, and he can like or dislike songs based on their colors.

Like all other synesthetes I've talked to, Day assumed everyone experienced what he did until as an eight-year-old boy, he mentioned the colors of a song he liked to his mother and realized she didn't know what he was talking about. As he says, "This didn't make me feel 'freakish' . . . or really bother me much at all. I would just not bother talking about my colored music to most people since I figured they wouldn't get it."

As he got older, however, he found that jazz musicians were sometimes good bets for getting it. Some of them had at least heard of musicians who experienced colored music—one thinks and wonders about the Miles Davis piece "Blue in Green" on his album *Kind of Blue*. Day, however, says that Davis was not a synesthete, but simply interested in the idea of combining color and music. He has, however, heard that Dizzy Gillespie really *did* hear music in color. Day reports that his parents once belonged to the same church as Dizzy Gillespie. They and other church members recall Gillespie describing his colored music in talks he sometimes gave to church members.

As for his own colored music, Day reports the colors of some songs arouse strong emotions for him. The hues of Pink Floyd's "Comfortably Numb" from *The Wall* album, for instance, are "really scary." He describes the song's "shiny black" background as "lit up sporadically by distant lightning flashes—blue-white electric plasma . . . with thin streams of red trickling here and there on the black surface."

While Sean Day has experienced synesthesia ever since he can remember, the word "synesthesia" was introduced to him only much later in life by one of his professors at Purdue. Later still, Day recalls that a capacity for experiencing colored taste opened up when he drank a very strong cup of espresso coffee for the first time. The taste of the espresso made him "see a pool of green oil." After that, other colored flavors kicked in: Steamed gingered squid made him see bright orange shaving foam; beef steak made him see blue.

In running his synesthesia list and his own home page, Sean Day sees his mission as informing the public about their synesthete fellow citizens. Like many researchers, he believes that a better understanding of synesthesia will lead to a better understanding of the brain and of how its different parts communicate with each other. Furthermore, Day means to spread the word about the harmlessness and possible usefulness of synesthesia so that synesthetic perception is not confused with hallucination. He reports a couple of cases where such confusion has had tragic results: One South American writer to the synesthesia list told of another synesthete diagnosed as schizophrenic and hospitalized after saying that words had colors; similarly, a clinical psychologist in Taiwan told of a case of a Japanese synesthete who was hospitalized after reporting he always heard colored sounds. In a similar vein, at a regional meeting of the American Synesthesia Association held in November 1999 at Yale University's Pierce Lab, one researcher told of a U.S. mother who reported her family doctor had suspected her little son of being schizophrenic after the boy said he heard alphabet letters in color.

In running the list, Day's original idea was to create a forum for synesthetes to ask neurologists, psychologists, and other experts about their perceptions. However, since so many different theories are in process, Day says he saw "the best thing to do was actually to listen to what the synesthetes were saying and try to work things out with them. Whereas I was originally hoping I could tap into various 'experts' for help with my dissertation, I almost immediately turned to tapping other synesthetes instead."

Day has taught English at Taiwan's National Central University since 1996 and hopes to do more research on synesthetic experiences of speakers of Chinese. He has done considerable research on synesthesia, analyzing and tabulating differences among synesthetes' colored-language perceptions and gender differences in synesthetic perceptions (so far, he has found no significant differences between male and female synesthetes).

To visit Sean Day's home page, go to http://www.ncu.edu.tw/ ~daysa/synesthesia.htm. To join the synesthesia list, write to Sean Day at daysa@cc.ncu.tw. At this writing, Sean Day has been invited to teach in the English department of Miami University in Ohio. He may be contacted through the university's Web site at www.muohio.edu.

Along with researcher Peter Grossenbacher and artist Carol Steen, Sean Day is on the board of the developing American Synesthesia Association, Incorporated (ASA, Inc.). ASA, Inc. is a registered not-for-profit, tax-exempt organization. ASA, Inc. has held annual meetings at places including the National Institutes of Health, the J. B. Pierce Lab at Yale University, and Princeton University. The very first meeting of the American Synesthesia Association was attended by just two people, Carol Steen and me, as we sat in her artist's loft in 1995 sipping tea and dreaming of the possibility of a developing synesthesia network culture. For a long time, Carol and I were ASA's only two members, but our community is growing. (For information about ASA, Inc., contact Carol Steen at rednote@infohouse.com.)

ASA, Inc. held its first national meeting, hosted by Greta Berman and Carol Steen, on May 19, 2001, at Princeton University in a campus building appropriately and colorfully called Green Hall. Synesthesia conferences have the distinction of being among the very few (if not the only) ones where scientists and those they study mix with equal status. Scientist-presenters politely apologized to their audience of synesthetes for using the term "normal" or "abnormal" when referring to nonsynesthetes and synesthetes, explaining that they were using these terms only in the statistical sense. (One wonders if synesthesia conferences could become models for other kinds of "study-of-human-behavior" conferences—could something be gained by having researchers and those they study mix in this way?) One conference attendee, Sarah Piekut, a synesthete who has constructed a synesthesia Web site (www.geocities.com/gothique chiq/ Syn.html), remarked that she had never in her life seen so many individualistic people gathered in one place. It could be that synesthetes who have chosen to explore their offbeat perceptions and researchers who have chosen to buck convention by making this traditionally marginal topic their main focus of study are of a particularly individualistic turn of mind.

The researchers presented a range of experimental studies: Dr. Eric Odgaard, who conducts research with Dr. Larry Marks at Yale University's Pierce Laboratory, discussed experiments with synesthetes involving the "stroop effect." He explained that the stroop effect is what happens when you slow down a person's response time by dividing his attention. Almost all people take longer, for example, to identify the color of the word "green" if it is written in red ink. In the same way, he found that synesthetes will take longer to identify the color of letters or numbers if they are written in colors differing from their own synesthetic ones. Noam Sagiv of the University of California at Berkeley talked about the binding problem in synesthesia. He described experiments he conducted showing how information might come together in synesthetes' minds to form their synesthetic perceptions. Dr. Peter Grossenbacher gave an overview of synesthesia research and talked about what synesthesia can offer humanity in the twenty-first century. Dr. Gail Martino talked about how knowledge of the workings of weak synesthesia can be used in product research and development.

Researcher Edward Hubbard, along with the dynamic and fiery Dr. Vilayanur Ramachandran of the University of California at San Diego, closed the conference by showing how the study of synesthesia could provide "a window into human nature"—insights into, for example, the human mind's penchant to create metaphor. Ramachandran said, "Scientists have often dismissed synesthesia, saying, 'Oh, these artists are just speaking metaphorically.'" In this way, he said, scientists fall victim to the scientific fallacy of answering one mystery of human behavior with another mystery of human behavior. "What does it mean to speak metaphorically?" Ramachandran asks. "That, in itself, is a mystery." He went on to point out that the study of synesthesia may help us to unravel that mystery, since among synesthetes' heterogeneous neural patterns is one showing heightened activity in the angular gyrus, a brain area that plays a key role in the making of metaphor.

Although scientists at the conference expressed a range of differing views, often engaging in lively but friendly debates, a common understanding united them: None had any doubt of the existence of synesthetic perception. A critical mass of evidence has now been accumulated, and synesthesia has arrived in the scientific research community. Debates at the conference centered on issues central to many areas in the study of human behavior: To what degree is synesthesia genetically predisposed, to what extent environmentally shaped? How does the perception form and reach conscious awareness?

Researchers from the social sciences and the arts also presented. Robert and Michele Root-Bernstein each gave talks about synesthesia's place in their concept of aesthetic cognition (discussed in part in Chapter Six of this book). Filmmaker Sheri Wills talked of synesthesia's role in the history of filmmaking and showed how sound and image were fused in her synesthetic film *Nocturne*. Natasha Lvovich, writer and synesthete, gave a reading from her book *The Multilingual Self*, and I read an excerpt from the book you're reading now. Synesthete Carrie Schultz informally talked of her work-in-progress *Chroma*, a video installation aimed at giving audiences a taste of what synesthetes see.

Those who missed the ASA, Inc. conference but would still like to have a taste of what synesthetes see (synesthetic pun intended) may go to "The Synesthetic Experience," the Massachusetts Institute of Technology (MIT) synesthesia site, one of the first to go up. MIT student Karen Chenausky, a colored-language synesthete working on research in the field, started the site to inform the public about synesthesia and also, through the wonders of computer technology, to give nonsynesthetes a glimpse of how those with colored-language synesthesia perceive alphabet letters. The idea of using synesthesia as a basis for developing user technology in a unique way also spurred on her interest. In 1995, after obtaining a grant from MIT's Council for the Arts, Chenausky invited techie Steve Mann (of Webcam fame) and synesthetic artist Carol Steen to help design the site and to include slides of Steen's synesthetic-inspired paintings and sculpture. By 1997, the site, which is quite visually appealing and informative, had the distinction of being awarded two stars (out of a possible four; most sites receive no stars) by the prestigious *Encyclopedia Britannica*'s Web rating system. In the site's audio portion, Carol and Karen talk about their experiences of first discovering their synesthesia. In another part, visitors can click on ordinary black-printed words in a sentence and see them transform into Karen's synesthetically colored vision of alphabet letters.

Chenausky feels it's important for people to know about synesthesia because, as she says, "From a scientific standpoint, it's important to know how lots of people's minds work. Studying people with special abilities or disabilities is a time-honored way of investigating the mind in general." She also feels that understanding the compelling features of synesthetes' inner worlds has implications for making the interface between PC and PC users more pleasurable. To check out the site, go to http://web.mit.edu/synesthesia/www/synesthesia.html.

A European site that shows a number of synesthetic visions (colored alphabets, calendars, numbers, and the like) was created by two German synesthetes, Andreas Mengel and Angela Mehder. This site invites synesthetes to submit representations of their synesthetic perceptions (uniquely colored and configured alphabets, number trails, week and year pathways), which visitors can see by clicking on the gallery portion of the site. If you have (or can download) Flash Player 4, you can hear a recording of a radio program where I interview synesthetic artist Carol Steen and synesthesia researcher Peter

Grossenbacher (first broadcast on WNYE-FM, New York City's educational radio station). Mengel first had the idea to create a synesthesia Web site and did so with fellow synesthete Mehder because, as Angela says, "We both thought that the subject was ideal for the Internet—you can reach people around the world without expensive printing material or media campaigns." Mengel, who has a Ph.D. in phonetics and currently works as a database manager for a mobile phone company, experiences colored numbers and colored and shaped time units. He feels that the mind creates such visions because "we cannot directly perceive weeks and numbers, so we invent perceptions we can map onto them." Andreas felt impressed as he discovered the staggering array of number, letter, and time conceptualizations among synesthetes and felt there ought to be a database to store them. When he met Mehder, also a synesthete, they collaborated on making it a reality. Mehder comes from a family of female synesthetes. Since her mother and her two sisters always knew exactly what she meant when she described her colored numbers (although the colors of her numbers were different from the colors of theirs), she thought her classmates would as well. As little girls, Andrea and her sisters asked their classmates about their colored numbers and letters and discovered that, although most had no idea what they meant, a few of them "knew exactly what we were talking about," particularly one little girl, "who was good at playing music and had colored musical notes." Mehder herself finds that she is good at remembering long sequences of numbers, including telephone numbers. To visit Angela and Andreas's site, go to www.sensequence.de/indexen.html.

In Australia, Pat Higgs, a health and rehabilitation professional who is also synesthetic, decided to make a synesthesia home page after she learned there was a word for the colored voices and music she had always experienced. As Pat says, "It was a tremendous relief to know I was normal and that the color experiences were not some form of madness." Having a sense of community responsibility, Pat decided to work toward reaching other synesthetes and those in the helping professions with this information. The need for this became clear after she interviewed a number of mental health professionals and found only one with any knowledge of the phenomenon. As Pat says, "It would really be sad if there were other people like me who, because of lack of knowledge, were isolated with no one with whom to share information about [synesthetic] perceptions." Pat describes some of her more profound color music experiences, which she says she has during rare quiet hours in the evening while improvising on the piano: "I see emerald green circular shapes on or near the tips of my fingers. When this occurs, I am aware of feeling very serene and at peace within." At this writing, Pat Higgs's Web site is at http://www.traralgon.net/isa-aus/index.html.

ASA, Inc. was inspired by the International Synesthesia Association (ISA), started by researchers at Cambridge University in England. For several years running, ISA organized an annual Synesthesia Day, where researchers and synesthetes made presentations on their respective experiments and experiences. The ISA offers research articles and an annual newsletter of synesthesia news on its Web site. To visit the ISA site, go to www.psychiatry.cam.ac.uk/isa. To visit the ASA, Inc. site, go to www.multimediaplace.com/asa/.

You can also visit these other synesthesia sites, active at the time of this writing:

http://www.app.org/neuroman

http://www.doctorhugo.org/synaesthesia/

http://home.alphastar.de.VilenOi

http://www.sightings.com/ufo6/med.htm

http://www.macalester.edu/~psych/whathap/UBNRP/synesthesia/main.html

http://www.ozemail.com.au/~ddiamond/synth.html

http://adaweb.walkerart.org/partners/

http://avoca.vicnet.net.au/~colourmusic/

http://psyche.cs.monash.edu.au/psycheindexv2.html

A number of video and radio programs as well as books have covered the topic of synesthesia. Some are listed below:

TELEVISION AND VIDEO
Beyond the Human Senses, a British Broadcasting Company (BBC) production, July 11, 2000.

Orange Sherbet Kisses, a BBC production, December 13, 1994.

"Seeing Things," *60 Minutes* (Australia), April 12, 1998.

"The Strange World of Synesthesia," *Future Watch* (CNN), November 25, 1995.

Yellow Fridays (a documentary by Porter Gale of Stanford University; available free of charge to nonprofit groups and for $9.95 + $3.00 shipping to all others).

RADIO
Interview with Dr. Richard Cytowic, National Public Radio (NPR), 1993.

Interview with Dr. Richard Cytowic and Carol Steen, ABC Radio, *National Health Report,* July 1996.

Pat Duffy's Interview with Dr. Peter Grossenbacher and synesthetic artist Carol Steen, WNYE-FM (New York City educational radio), November 1999.

"Synesthesia in the Morning," Sebastian King's introduction of Pat Duffy and Natasha Lvovich, who gave readings from their respective books on synesthesia, *Blue Cats* and *The Multilingual Self,* WNYE-FM, New York, September 2000.

Interview with Dr. Peter Grossenbacher and synesthete Carol Crane, *Todd Mundt Show,* NPR, 2000.

"Synesthesia," with host John Hockenberry; interviews with researchers and synesthetes (including Dmitri Nabokov), *The Infinite Mind,* NPR, January 14, 2001.

FICTION

Joris-Karl Huysmann, *Against Nature.*

Vladimir Nabokov, *The Gift.*

Vladimir Nabokov, *Ada.*

Katherine Vaz, *Saudade.*

Boris Vian, *Mood Indigo.*

RECENT NONFICTION

Richard Cytowic, *Synaesthesia: A Union of the Senses.* (As of this writing, a revised version of Dr. Cytowic's 1989 book was expected out in fall 2001.)

John Harrison, *Synaesthesia: The Strangest Thing.*

Leonardo on-line bibliography, "Synesthesia in Art and Science": http://mitpress.mi.edu/e-journals/Leonardo/isast/spec.projects/ synesthesiabib.htm (includes articles mentioned here, such as Carol Steen's "A Vision Shared" and Greta Berman's "Synesthesia and the Arts")

Other books and articles on synesthesia can be found in the Bibliography.

As I watch the programs, read the books, and log on to the Internet sites, I think of my father—and I realize I'm continuing the conversation with him that began back in 1968.

Long before the Internet existed and prestigious universities dignified the study of synesthesia with conferences and Web sites, my father, all by himself, validated what I saw. Because he was convinced there was some sense to his daughter's unusual perceptions, he was able to engage in that suspension of disbelief needed for one vision to open to another, and by so doing continue the endless process of diversifying and transforming that is the business of living.

Nature, so endlessly creative, has arranged things so that each of us, synesthete or nonsynesthete, perceives a slightly different world. Each time any of us looks at the world, a new world is created, a world colored by our one-of-a-kind patterns of neurons and experiences. Logged on to the Internet, that growing cyber-world of all of humanity's diverse visions, I can still hear my father say, "Patty, isn't it amazing?"

acknowledgments

First, I'd like to thank my husband, Josh Cohen, for his unending, unswerving, and often unbelievable love, patience, and support for me and this project—no matter where on the globe he happened to be. This book would never have been written if Josh had not come across an article on synesthesia in *The Economist* magazine back in 1993 and passed it to me, asking casually, "Isn't this what you have?" My excitement at discovering that renewed synesthesia research was taking place led me to make a "pilgrimage" to London to meet renowned neuroscientist Dr. Simon Baron-Cohen, now of Cambridge University. I thank Dr. Baron-Cohen for meeting and taking tea with me that day and for answering all my many questions about synesthesia.

Other researchers I would like to thank are Dr. Larry Marks, Director of the J. B. Pierce Laboratory at Yale University. I thank him for taking time out of his very busy schedule to read and comment on the manuscript of this book. I also thank him for writing the original 1975 *Psychology Today* article that first introduced me to synesthesia and kindled my interest in learning more. Thanks also to Dr. Gail Martino, who conducted synesthesia research with Dr. Marks, for taking time to read and give helpful and encouraging feedback on the manuscript of this book; a big thank you also to Dr. Michael Dickson for reading and commenting on my manuscript and for the hospitality he showed in inviting me to visit a site of synesthesia research at the University of Waterloo in Ontario, Canada. A great thank you to Dr. Richard Cytowic, whose ground-breaking research on synesthesia and courage to buck convention showed the importance of what had been considered a "fringe" area of study. A very special thank you to Dr. Peter Grossenbacher for inviting me to the "synesthesia" laboratory at the National Institutes of Health and for his continuing pioneering work on synesthesia studies at Naropa University; I thank him for his comments on this manuscript, for his willingness to answer questions about synesthesia, and, of course, for his friendship.

I would like to thank my family members for their support: Luna Tarlo, my mother-in-law, friend, and fellow writer, for her unwavering interest and moral support; thanks also to the Duffy clan (Henry, Mary, Matthew, and James) for their loving interest in this project; a big thank you to my sister-in-law, E. Marie Duffy for her ever-present love and support.

I extend a very big and special thank you to my niece, Christina Duffy, and to my nephew, Sean Duffy, for reading key chapters of this book and providing helpful feedback on them.

A great thank you to Faye Bender for her kindness, competence, and professionalism, and for believing in this project and making it happen; of course, a sincere thank you to Amy Yee for her friendship, support, and special gift of bringing people together. I thank my editor, John Michel, for his enthusiasm for this project and his editorial suggestions, most especially the one that prompted me to think more about my relationship with my father. I would also like to thank Rosalind Palermo Stevenson and Laura Glenn for their great friendship and invaluable fellow-writerly support; for their encouragement, Karyn Meyer, Odile Kory, Anna Muir, and the entire Muir family; a special thanks to my friend Jim Tamulis for providing articles, suggestions, and confidence in this project. A special thanks, too, to my first synesthete-friend, Ann Kennedy; a very big thanks to my friend and fellow synesthete, Carol Steen, for dreaming with me about a synesthete network culture and making it come true. Thanks to the ever-inspiring Enid Holt Harper and to the ever-energetic Sebastain King; a sincere thanks to Bhikshuni Weisbrot of the United Nations Society of Writers for her friendship and support.

Finally, I would like to thank the late Allan Kent Dart, my great friend and writing mentor, whose humor and appreciation of the off-beat bathed this project in his own special sunlight.

bibliography

Ackerman, Diane. 1990. *A Natural History of the Senses.* New York: Vintage.

Baron-Cohen, S., and Harrison, J. 1997. *Synaesthesia: Classic and Contemporary Essays.* Oxford: Blackwell Publishers.

Baron-Cohen, S., Wyke, M., and Binnie, C. 1988. "Hearing Words and Seeing Colors: An Experimental Investigation of a Case of Synaesthesia." *Perception* 16, 761–767.

Baudelaire, Charles. 1971. *Artificial Paradise.* New York: Herder and Herder.

Benson, Herbert. 1966. *Timeless Healing.* New York: Scribner's.

Berman, Greta. 1999. "Synesthesia and the Arts." *Leonardo: Journal for the International Society for the Arts, Sciences, and Technology.* The MIT Press, vol. 32, no. 1, 15–22.

Birren, F. 1978. *Color and Human Response.* New York: John Wiley & Sons Inc.

Blakeslee, Sandra. 1991. "Brain Yields New Clues on Its Organization for Language." *New York Times,* September 10, C1.

———. 2000. "'Rewired' Ferrets Overturn Theory of Brain Growth." *New York Times,* April 25, F1.

Csikszentmihalyi, Mihaly. *Flow: The Psychology of Optimal Experience.* New York: Harper Collins.

Cytowic, Richard. 1989. *Synaesthesia: A Union of the Senses.* New York: Springer-Verlag.

———. 1993. *The Man Who Tasted Shapes.* New York: Tarcher/Putnam.

Dann, K. 1998. *Bright Colors Falsely Seen.* New Haven, CT: Yale University Press.

Dehaene, Stanislav. 1997. *The Number Sense.* New York: Oxford University Press.

Dixon, Michael, and Merikle, Philip. 2000. "5 + 2 = Yellow." *Nature* 406 (July), 365.

Feynman, Richard. 1988. *What Do You Care What Other People Think? Further Adventures of a Curious Character.* New York: Norton.

Gardner, Howard. 1993. *Multiple Intelligences.* New York: Basic Books.

Goode, Erica. 1999. "When People Hear a Color and See a Sound." *New York Times*, February, F3.

Grossenbacher, Peter. 1997. "Perception and Information in Synaesthetic Experience." In *Synaesthesia: Classic and Contemporary Essays*, ed. Simon Baron-Cohen and John Harrison. Oxford, UK, and Cambridge, USA: Blackwell.

Grossenbacher, P. G., and Lovelace, C. T. 2001. "Mechanisms of Synesthesia: Cognitive and Physiological Constraints," *Trends in Cognitive Sciences* 5:1, 36–41.

Harrison, John, and Baron-Cohen, S. 1995. "Synaesthesia: Reconciling the Subjective with the Objective." *Elsevier Science Ltd.*, 157–160.

Horiuchi, Toshimi. 1980. *The Minnesota Poems.* Tokyo: The Hokuseido Press.

Hornick, Sue. 2001. "For Some, Pain Is Orange." *Smithsonian Magazine* (February), 48–54.

Juster, Norton. 1964. *The Phantom Toll Booth.* New York: Random House.

Kosslyn, S. M., Ball, T. M., and Reiser, B. J. 1978. "Visual Images Preserve Metric Spatial Information: Evidence from Studies of Image Scanning," *Journal of Experimental Psychology: Human Perception* 4:1, 47–60.

Kubin, Alfred. 1968. *Alfred Kubin's Autobiography.* New York: Galerie St. Etienne.

Lemley, Brad. 1999. "Do You See What They See?" *Discover Magazine* (December), 80–87.

Lewkowicz, David, and Turkewitz, Gerald. 1981. "Intersensory Interaction in Newborns: Modification of Visual Preferences Following Exposure to Sound." *Child Development* 52, 827–832.

Lim, Jay Alan (composer). 2000. Quoted in Program Notes, San Francisco Symphony Orchestra performance of *Rough Magic* (April).

Lusseyran, Jacques. 1998. *And There Was Light*. New York: Parabola Books. [Orig. Little, Brown & Co., 1963.]

Lvovich, Natasha. 1997. *The Multilingual Self*. Mahwah, NJ: Lawrence Erlbaum Associates.

Macklin, Elizabeth. 2000. "Midnight Blue." In *You've Just Been Told*. New York: Norton.

Marks, Lawrence. 1997. "On Colored Hearing Synesthesia." In *Synaesthesia: Classic and Contemporary Essays*, ed. Simon Baron-Cohen and John Harrison. Oxford, UK, and Cambridge, USA: Blackwell.

Martino, Gail, and Marks, Lawrence. 1999. "Perceptual and Linguistic Interactions in Speeded Classification: Tests of the Semantic Coding Hypothesis." *Perception* 28, 903–923.

———. 2001. "Synesthesia: Strong and Weak." *Current Directions in Psychological Science* 10, no. 2 (April), 61–65.

Maurer, Daphne, and Maurer, Charles. 1988. *The World of the Newborn*. New York: Basic Books.

Motluck, Alison. 1993. "Purple Prose." *The Economist*, September 4.

———. 1997. "Two Synaesthetes Talking Color." In *Synaesthesia: Classic and Contemporary Essays*, ed. Simon Baron-Cohen and John Harrison. Oxford, UK, and Cambridge, USA: Blackwell, 270–277.

Nabokov, Vladimir. 1947. *Speak, Memory*. New York: Random House.

Paulescu, E., Harrison, J., Baron-Cohen, S., et al. 1995. "The Physiology of Colored Hearing." *Brain* 118, 661–676.

Pinker, Stephen. 1994. *The Language Instinct: How the Mind Creates Language*. New York: William Morrow and Company.

Root-Bernstein, Robert, and Root-Bernstein, Michele. 1999. *Sparks of Genius: Thirteen Thinking Tools of the World's Most Creative People*. Boston and New York: Houghton-Mifflin.

Sacks, Oliver. 1995. *An Anthropologist on Mars*. New York: Vintage.

Salzman, Mark. 2000. *Lying Awake*. New York: Knopf.

Sitwell, Edith. 1954. *Collected Poems*. New York: Vanguard Press.

Steen, Carol. 2001. "A Vision Shared." *Leonardo: Journal for the International Society for the Arts, Sciences, and Technology*. The MIT Press, vol. 34, no. 3 (June), 203–208.

Watson, Ian. "The Common Triggers of Synesthesia Are Social Conventions." Paper presented at the Central States Anthropology Society Meeting, Milwaukee, Wisconsin, April 1997.

Wheeler, Raymond, and Cutsforth, Thomas. 1922. *The Synesthesia of a Blind Subject*. Eugene: University of Oregon.

———. 1922. "Synesthesia: A Form of Perception." *Psychological Review* 29, 212–220.

index

Subjectivity, perceptual, 31–32, 58–59, 76–78
Superior temporal gyrus, in synesthesia, 130
Synesthesia
  acquired, 43–44
  age-related loss of, 11, 138
  in animals, 63
  attentional focus in, 112–118
  in children, 11–13, 17–19, 42, 138–139
  classification of, 42–50
  colored-letter, 1–3, 19–25. See also Colored-letter synesthesia
  colored-music, 39, 40, 79–82, 89, 99–108. See also Musical synesthesia
  colored-number, 41, 69–75, 105–106. See also Colored-number synesthesia
  common features of, 5
  conceptual, 147
  conceptual aspects of, 140–141
  conferences on, 162–166
  as conscious process, 102–104
  constitutional, 42n, 47
  continuum of, 46–50
  definition of, xi, 2
  developmental, 42, 47
  drug-induced, 44–50
  early research on, 4, 25–26, 34, 41–42
  evolutionary benefit of, 29, 144–145
  as form of thinking, 151
  forms of, 19–32
  genetic factors in, 2, 5, 26–29
  gustatory, 160–161

  idiopathic, 42n, 47
  in infants, 11–13
  as integrative experience, 107–108
  lay attitudes toward, 61–63
  in males vs. females, 26, 27, 30, 162
  metaphorical, 42–43
  musical, 39, 40, 79–82, 89, 99–108, 115–116, 159–160. See also Musical synesthesia
  professional attitudes toward, 63–64
  Romantic movement and, 38–41
  skepticism about, 62–64
  strong, 49–50
  subjectivity of, 31–32, 58–59, 76–78
  trauma-related loss of, 120
  weak, 48–50
Synesthesia: A Union of the Senses (Cytowic), 20, 82, 115
Synesthesia: Classic and Contemporary Readings (Baron-Cohen & Harrison), 63
"Synesthesia: Reconciling the Subjective with the Objective" (Harrison & Baron-Cohen), 31
"Synesthesia: Strong and Weak" (Marks), 49–50
Synesthesia list, 159–162
The Synesthesia of a Blind Subject (Wheeler), 44
Synesthetic art, 53–54, 56–57, 113–116, 145–146
"The Synesthetic Experience" (MIT Web site), 164–165

Tactile learning, 143
Tactile qualities, of colors, 43–44

illustration credits

about the author

PATRICIA DUFFY's essays and articles have appeared in *The San Francisco Chronicle, New York Newsday, The Village Voice, The Boston Globe, The Philadelphia Inquirer, Ms.,* and many other magazines and newspapers. Her work is also to be included in the anthologies *They Only Laughed Later: Tales of Women on the Move* and *Soulful Living.* She is also a cofounder of and a consultant to the American Synesthesia Association.